# MILLER'S

## COLLECTING
# TEXTILES

**Miller's Collecting Textiles**
**Patricia Frost**

First published in Great Britain in 2000 by Miller's
a division of Octopus Publishing Group Ltd
2–4 Heron Quays
Docklands
London E14 4JP

Miller's is a registered trademark of Octopus Publishing
Group Ltd

© 2000 Octopus Publishing Group Ltd

Commissioning Editor **Anna Sanderson**
Project Editors **John Jervis and Mary Scott**
Executive Art Editor **Vivienne Brar**
Art Editors **Rhonda Fisher and Lucy Parissi**
Editor **Caroline Behr**
Design **SteersMcGillan Ltd**
Picture Research **Maria Gibbs**
Proofreader **Miranda Stoner**
Index **Hilary Bird**
Production **Nancy Roberts**

The publishers will be grateful for any information that will assist
them in keeping future editions up to date. While every care has
been taken in the preparation of this book, neither the author nor
the publisher can accept any liability for any consequence arising
from the use thereof, or the information contained therein.

ISBN 1 84000 203 4

A CIP record for this book is available from the British Library

Set in Helvetica Neue and Granjon
Produced by Toppan Printing Co., (HK) Ltd
Printed and bound in China

Half-title:
A raised work mirror, embroidered on ivory silk,
English, 17th century.
Title:
An embroidered quilted waistcoat, English, 18th century.

746

# COLLECTING
# TEXTILES

**Patricia Frost**

# The Author

Patricia Frost joined Christie's after university, and is now
an Associate Director and Head of Ceramics. She
is a member of the BBC's *Antiques Roadshow* team,
and set up the popular Street Fashion sales at Christie's,
featuring costumes and accessories from the 1960s
and 1970s. She is currently specializing in Oriental and
Islamic Textiles, and writes for *Antique Collector* magazine.
She also contributed to *The Illustrated History of Textiles*
edited by Madeleine Ginsburg.

# The Contributors

Alison Toplis completed an MA in the History of Dress at
the Courtauld Institute of Art, London, in 1993. She was
employed at Christie's, London, from 1994 to 1999, where
she specialized in European costume and textiles. She now
works on a freelance basis.

Janie Lightfoot has run the Textile Conservation and
Restoration Studio in London for 23 years. She works on
major costume and textile collections, mounts exhibitions
in Britain and abroad, and conserves and maintains collections of costume and textiles for museums, historic houses,
the Church and private individuals. She also lectures to
educational institutions and societies on conservation and
restoration practice.

# Contents

# Introduction

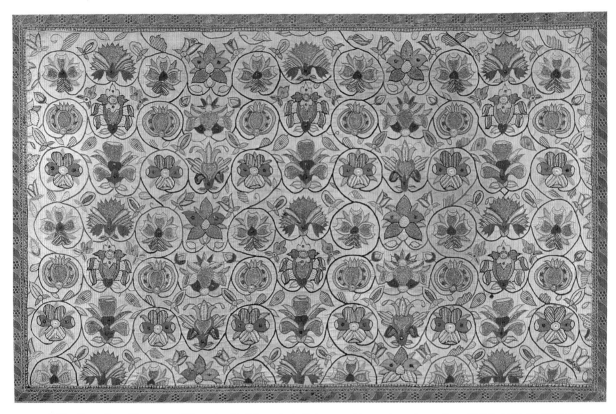

▲ **Needlework cushion cover** 17th-century English, worked with honeysuckle, pansies and carnations. £1,500–2,000/$2,400–3,200

This book is intended to introduce the reader to the variety of textiles available to the collector on the open market. Whether your taste is for the domestic embroideries of 17th-century Britain, or for the elegance of Rococo France, I hope to provide you with a basic guide of what to look out for and what is available. This book concentrates on the 17th to 20th centuries and is divided into chapters by technique, including embroideries, woven silks and beadwork. There are separate chapters on items such as shawls and laces which are defined collectors' interests. The book also contains a short history of the more recent phenomenon of designer textiles, from William Morris to Lucienne Day.

## Why collect?

One of the most appealing things about textiles is their ability to bridge the gap in imagination between our times and the past. The lustre of 18th-century silk damask is easily appreciated in the 20th century, without the need for any historical knowledge. Learning about a textile's history will, however, still enhance its appeal. For example, being aware that the cost of lace in the 17th century was roughly equivalent to the cost of fine jewels explains why the young ladies of the day lavished so much attention on the embroidered caskets they worked to store their frills and flounces. Both caskets and laces are still widely available today. Holding a lady's lace cap or a sampler embroidered by a young girl in the 17th century can, in an instant, take you back in time, sometimes at relatively little expense. This book is intended to guide the reader through the many and various collecting fields, pointing out the highlights on the way and giving hints on finding both bargains and museum pieces.

### Where to look

Auction rooms regularly provide a selection of textiles which are available to be viewed and, most importantly, touched and examined at length. Auction-house staff will usually be happy to advise on the pieces in their sales and can prove valuable guides to new collectors – it is worthwhile cultivating a relationship. You also have the reassurance of knowing that the auction houses stand by their catalogue descriptions.

Dealers in antique textiles are mainly but not exclusively concentrated around the larger cities, particularly London and New York. However, there are notable exceptions. The advantage of regularly visiting your local dealers lies in the fact that they will generally have more time to find out your likes and dislikes, whereas viewing at auction rooms is necessarily limited by time. Eventually, a good dealer should be able to judge your taste, and will often go to some lengths to find the perfect piece for a good customer. Reputable dealers also guarantee their goods and some undertake to take back pieces they have sold. You should enquire, when purchasing, what the dealer offers in this respect.

Specialist fairs are an excellent way of cutting down on the amount of legwork required to pursue your interest. Prices are generally slightly higher, to reflect the effort put in by the exhibitors in sourcing the goods. Your level of protection is correspondingly high. Jumble sales also offer the collector the opportunity of finding hidden treasure. A little knowledge will go a long way at a jumble sale. You obviously have far less protection and will have to back up your instincts with hard cash. However, the thrill of the hunt is not to be discounted.

E-commerce is fast becoming a factor in this collectors' market. Numerous sites and dealers now use the Web to advertise and sell textiles. The level of protection for the buyer varies from site to site but probably is similar to buying at a smaller fair or jumble sale. You should read the conditions of sale very carefully on each site.

### Values

While the majority of textiles on the market are priced at relatively modest rates, you should be aware that certain specialist areas command very high prices – a 16th-century Persian velvet can realize over £750,000 ($1,200,000) at auction. Auction houses offer a very useful free verbal valuation service, either by appointment or by looking at photographs. Museums will offer advice on origin and date, but are not generally allowed to suggest values. The best advice is to get a second opinion before laying out larger sums.

### What you should know before buying

The more experience you have of looking at textiles, the less likely you are to make a mistake. Visit your local museum, and specialist museums such as the Victoria & Albert Museum, London. Handle as many pieces as you can, either in salerooms or in dealers' showrooms. You will be building up a mental picture of the correct texture and colour which will be invaluable for the day when you find an unexpected treasure.

Knowledge of the structures of textiles will be a great help in making decisions. I have found trying to weave a simple band on a child's toy loom very instructive. You might also try taking up a needle and thread so that you can understand the skill involved in stitching a sampler.

The best advice one can receive is to follow one's natural inclinations when assembling a collection. There are those who diligently put together exhaustive collections for the purpose of investment, but most collect out of obsession. This drives them out of bed on cold winter mornings, to stand in queues at antiques fairs while the rest of us are still pulling on our coats.

Finally, one should always purchase what you really love. You have to live with what you buy, so I hope this book will give you some useful hints and helpful information to back up the choices you make.

# Techniques: Embroidery

## The basic stitches used to create complex designs and beautiful fabrics across the world

▲ **Embroidered nightcap**
An English embroidered gentleman's
nightcap from the early 17th century.
£10,000–15,000/$16,000–24,000

Embroidery is a simple technique which involves the most basic of equipment – a needle and thread. Superb quality is a question of skill and fineness of stitch, rather than complicated machinery unavailable to the amateur. It is therefore one of the few crafts in which the amateur and professional can compete on equal terms if the basic stitches below are mastered.

Being able to recognize stitches is useful to the collector as it gives hints as to where embroideries may have been produced. Most are relatively simple in theory, but rather more tricky in execution. The fineness of the embroidery and its value to the collector is entirely based on the skill of the needlewoman and the success of her design. Embroideries of great skill but little design merit are rarely in demand. For example, photographically realistic Japanese embroidery of the late 19th century is as yet of little commercial value. The piece that combines both great skill and great design is what the collector really wants.

Cross stitch (*see* fig.1) is the most basic method of covering the surface of a textile, and is the only stitch used for Berlin woolwork (*see* pp.28–9). It was also commonly used for needlework carpets from the 17th century onwards, as a durable and quick ground stitch. The southern Italians and the Greeks use the same stitch with a twist to the centre.

Satin stitch is another simple stitch in which the embroidery threads are worked in flat, straight lines. It is used on embroidered pictures, coverlets and samplers throughout the world.

Couched stitch (*see* fig.2) is an economical way of placing all the expensive embroidery thread on the front of the fabric where it will be seen, without wasting any on the reverse. In times when real gold was used as an embroidery thread, and when silks were goods imported at great cost from the East, this was a particular advantage. A second advantage of this stitch is that it rapidly covers large areas of fabric. Threads are laid on the cloth and tacked

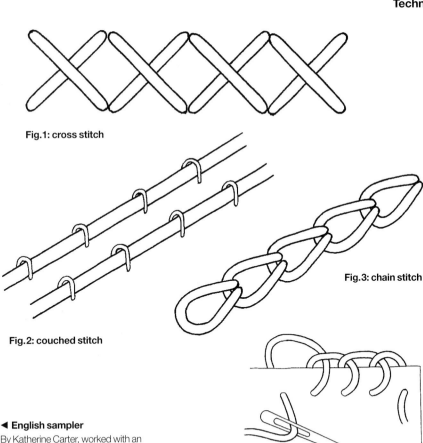

**Fig.1: cross stitch**

**Fig.2: couched stitch**

**Fig.3: chain stitch**

**Fig.4: buttonhole stitch**

◀ **English sampler**
By Katherine Carter, worked with an alphabet and rows of variations of undulating flower stems, 17th century.
£500–800/$800–1,300

down at right angles with a self-coloured thread at intervals – this technique is used almost exclusively with metal threads that are expensive and difficult to thread through a needle and through cloth.

Raised work or stumpwork is a variation of couched stitching in which a layer of wadding is laid underneath the couched thread, creating a third dimension. However, the Jacobeans would not have understood the term stumpwork, which was invented in the 19th century, so today this technique is generally know as raised work. The same method was used extensively in the 18th and 19th centuries in southern Europe and the Ottoman Empire on gilt embroideries.

Chain stitch (*see* fig.3) was used extensively in India, Turkey and Iran but was also produced in the 18th century in Beauvais, France. It continued to be popular in the 19th century, and it is also known as tambour work in this period, because it was worked by

stretching fabric tightly over a frame or drum (*tambour* in French), and piercing it with a sharp hook to pull the thread through the fabric. Mechanical versions of this stitch appear from the 19th century. If there are two separate threads, one on the right side and one on the reverse, the work has been done by machine.

Buttonhole stitch (*see* fig.4) is a staple of dressmaking and embroidery. It is used to finish off raw edges such as buttonholes but can also be used as a decorative stitch when the stitches are built up in rows. Patterns are created by leaving gaps in the stitches. The detached buttonhole stitch is found as early as the 12th century in China – it is known as needle looping in this context. In this Chinese work, flat gilt strips of paper are often laid behind coloured silk buttonhole stitches, so that gold shimmers through the pattern holes. The same stitch is used in 18th-century English Hollie Point on plain white linen or cotton, and as the centres for many flowers on needle laces.

# Techniques: Silk & Velvet

## The skilful and diverse weaving methods used to create a huge range of fabrics

All woven textiles are based on a warp and weft. The warp threads run up and down on the loom, the weft threads from left to right. The simplest fabric is a tabby, with a single warp and a single weft thread, passing alternately over and under each other (*see* fig.1) in a basket weave.

Satins are produced by showing more of the warp threads on the front of the fabric by passing the wefts under several warps (*see* fig.2) rather than over and under each pair. When a pattern is introduced into the weaving, the structure becomes more complex. The most common form of patterning is brocading (*see* fig.3). Brocades use a supplementary weft thread to form the pattern. It is not part of the structure and could in fact be removed without the fabric falling apart. When it is not required on the front of the fabric, it is left to float on the reverse.

The imprecise term "figured silk" is often used to describe patterns that are not brocaded. A figured silk might be a lampas, which is a silk that employs more than one set of warps and wefts. One set holds the structure together (binding warps and wefts) and the other is used to introduce pattern. The resulting silk is stronger than a brocade and can have a gold or silver ground, for example. Generally speaking, lampas weaves are used for complex figurative silks, and are usually, though not exclusively, an indicator of an early date.

Velvet is usually a tabby weave with a supplementary warp that has been caught up over a rod during weaving to form loops (*see* fig.4). The rod

**▲ Genoese velvet**
The patterns are shaved into the pile with considerable skill.
£500–800/$800–1,300

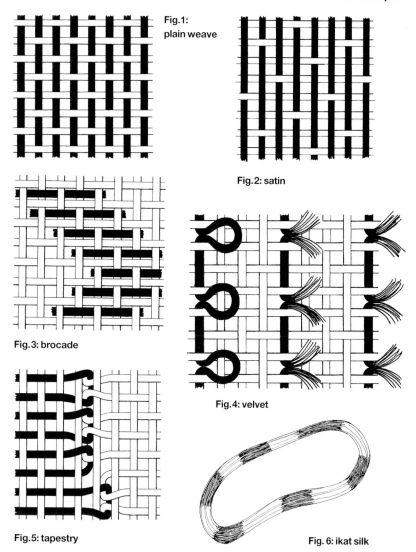

**Fig.1: plain weave**

**Fig.2: satin**

**Fig.3: brocade**

**Fig.4: velvet**

**Fig.5: tapestry**

**Fig.6: ikat silk**

is then removed. The loops are held in place by weft threads and can be cut to form pile velvet, or left uncut to form *ciselé* (uncut velvet). The length of the cut pile can be varied too, forming "two-pile velvet". Some velvets, especially Genoese ones, have a pattern incised into the pile with a razor.

Although often used to refer to embroidery, the word tapestry is a precise term for a woven technique. Tapestry weaving uses a straightforward warp structure but discontinuous wefts (*see* fig.5). Where one colour weft meets another, it does not continue on the reverse as brocade does, but turns back and completes another row. The way the colours interlock when they meet can be either dove-tailed, or left as a slit. This has to be hand-woven, so is primarily used for prestige fabrics such as tapestry wall-hangings

and Kashmir shawls, or for small-scale accessories such as purses. It is also used in weaving flat rugs in Turkey, India and Iran.

*Chiné* or ikat silks and cottons all introduce pattern by dying the warp threads before weaving (*see* fig.6). They look slightly fuzzy as it is virtually impossible to avoid some colour bleeding. The skill is therefore transferred from the weaver to the dyer. Skeins of thread are bound precisely where the dye is not to penetrate and dipped in vats of colour. The skeins are then carefully mounted on the loom in sequence. When both warps and wefts have been pre-dyed with a pattern, the cloth is known as double ikat. Considerable skill is needed to calculate the dyeing of both threads, and weaving has to be precise to avoid throwing the pattern out of line.

# Techniques: Lace

## The different techniques used in each of the major centres of lacemaking

**▲ Mechlin bobbin lace**
Showing the single thread *cordonnet* outline of motifs, and a variety of twisted fillings to the flowers, including leadlights. Mechlin lace is recorded as early as 1657, but this example dates from the 18th century.

To the untutored eye, the structure of lace can look extremely complicated. However, this is one of the rare occasions when technical knowledge will quickly open the doors to allowing you to understand where and how a piece of lace was made. Lacemakers always follow the same local rules – no improvisation is involved or welcomed. Analysing how a piece was made will therefore, more often than not, tell you where it was made and probably even when. Beginners should take heart, learn some basic techniques, and arm themselves with a magnifying glass.

The first thing to decide is whether your lace is a bobbin or needle lace. Needle laces will show recognizable stitches and will not have cloth-like centres to flowers. In the hand, bobbin laces usually feel floppier and more flexible than needle laces. The basic stitch for free-standing needle lace is the buttonhole stitch (*see* pp.8–9). The only equipment needed is a needle, thread, pins and parchment, and even the most complex needle lace flounce is produced in this way.

One of the earliest needle laces is cutwork. Holes are cut into linen ground, which is then oversewn in buttonhole stitch to prevent fraying. The diagonals of these square holes are then replaced by needle lace. This kind of lace is mainly found on linen table covers and altar cloths. Other needle laces of the late 16th and 17th centuries began as the decorative stitches linking seams, especially in shirt seams, although the technique continued well into the 19th century.

To decide whether the lace you are holding is a bobbin lace, you need to look through your magnifying glass at the densest areas of the lace. If this looks like a woven cotton under the loop, it is a bobbin lace. If it is made of buttonhole stitches, it is a needle lace. The basic technique of bobbin lace is plaiting and knotting. The bobbin lacemaker requires

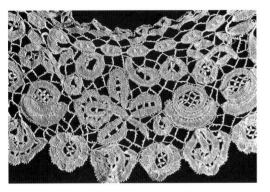

**▲ Honiton bobbin lace**
This 19th-century lace has the typical design of roses with cross-hatched tallies in the centre. Lozenge shapes along the top edge were produced by the yard.

**◄ Drawn threadwork**
Showing the original linen ground on the left, with a border composed of pulling out warps and wefts of the linen and binding the remainder together into a grid pattern. 17th century.

**▼ Argentan needle lace**
The clothwork is built up of rows of buttonhole stitches with characteristic hexagonal buttonholed net. 18th century.

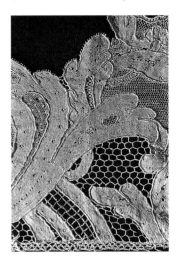

**◄ Alençon needle lace**
Each flower is outlined by a ridge of buttonhole stitches forming *picots* or points in this late 18th-century lace. The stitches would have been formed over horsehair, which is sometimes still present.

thread, a pillow on which to pin work in place, bobbins to weight the threads, and needles or stilettos to manipulate the threads and pins.

The simplest bobbin lace consists of plaiting, and peasant laces are as simple as this. The more complex the lace, the more a bobbin lace will resemble a woven cloth. Bobbin lace reached its zenith in the mid-18th century with the Flemish laces of Binche, Valenciennes and Brabant, which can look as if they are embroidered linen when viewed from a distance.

The woven areas of bobbin lace are known as *toilé* or clothwork. Half stitch is a way of introducing shading into clothwork. Being less dense, it looks darker than the surrounding areas. *Picots* are the small knops produced by several buttonhole stitches being sewn into the same hole on the edge of a motif. *Cordonnets* are single or double threads outlining the motifs, as in Mechlin lace, for example. In Brussels lace, however, the motifs are outlined only by a ridge of clothwork.

Wheatears and tallies are oval or square-ended, and are formed by working several threads together. Maltese lace has large silk oval wheatears, while Honiton has square-ended tallies often used in cross-hatched formation in the centre of roses and thistles. In Honiton these are known as "leadlights".

Lace techniques may pose problems to the novice for some time – the most productive method of identifying a lace is to arm yourself with a book and search for an illustration and description matching the piece. Since lacemakers rarely deviated from the particular local stitches, most laces will be identifiable if you can read the technical evidence. The occasional lace was made by mavericks who disregarded local custom and experimented with new variants – even the greatest lace experts occasionally admit defeat in the face of such pieces. In time, however, you will be able to identify at a glance where a lace comes from, without even needing to reach for your magnifying glass.

# Embroidery

## From the 17th to the 19th century: beautifully worked pieces from Britain, America and the Continent

▲ **Casket, purse and quill holder, by J.H., 1666**
Typical of styles of the late 1660s, the quality is extraordinarily high. The price of such an embroidered casket rises considerably when the initials of the embroiderer are recorded, as here on the purse. **£80,000–150,000/$128,000–240,000** for the set

The English have a very long and distinguished history of needlework stretching back to the Middle Ages. *Opus Anglicanum*, literally "English work" was world renowned. Exclusively ecclesiastical, and embroidered by nuns, some splendid vestments and altarcloths have survived. Occasionally a fragment will turn up at auction. Until the 17th century, the Church was the most important patron of needlework, Then a shift in emphasis occurred towards the domestic. Modern collectors have to remember that women of all social classes were required to sew at the very least their own trousseau, if not the clothes of the entire family. From a very young age, young girls were set to work on their samplers, instilling in them an early love of embroidery. Building on this groundwork, English 17th-century domestic embroidery reached a high point of technical brilliance and charm. Many of these domestic pieces survive and appear regularly on the market.

First-class embroideries from the early part of the 17th century are rare, and mainly survive in the form of caps, also known as coifs, with their associated triangular forehead covers;

stomachers, which formed part of a lady's bodice over which the decorative lacing was pinned; and the occasional pair of gloves. Entire bodices, jackets or petticoats are very rare, as successive generations are always tempted to refashion old embroideries into something more contemporary. Very often, only fragments remain.

These early 17th-century embroideries are typically worked in silks and metal threads on a fine linen ground. Stitches are various, including satin, split and buttonhole stitch, and any form of raised or three-dimensional work is highly prized. Occasionally, novelties such as a three-dimensional spray of flowers or a needle case in the shape of a frog appear on the market, and can fetch prices in four figures.

Variants on the coloured embroideries include the ever-popular "blackwork", worked entirely in black with gold and silver highlights, and embroideries in monochrome red which are also much prized.

The flowers that are worked into these pieces are those so popular with Elizabethans and Jacobeans: carnation, rose, sweet pea, strawberry and honeysuckle. Most could be found in a typical knot garden of the time.

**▼ Raised work mirror-cover**
The closed doors are worked with two men, symbolizing the old world and the new. The animals in each corner represent the four continents. Typical of the late 17th century.
**£20,000–40,000/$32,000–6,400**

**▲ Embroidered cushion**
Probably used for carrying a Bible in the early 17th century. **£1,500–2,000/$2,400–3,200**

**◄ Gentleman's night cap**
Trimmed with gold lace and embroidered with foliage, typical of the early 17th century. Examples in excellent condition such as this are rare. **£15,000–20,000/$23,000–32000**

Many, like the carnation, had medicinal uses, as well as being part of the language of courtship. They also recall sweetness either of taste or smell in an age which was not known for its oral hygiene or regular bathing.

By the middle of the 17th century, the floral coils of the earlier part of the century were making way for narrative embroideries. Survivors of this time include a large number of embroidered pictures in satin, counted and couched stitches, the ground of cream satin. The subject matter is often improving and taken from the Old Testament, for example Susannah and the Elders; or from classical mythology, such as Judith and the head of Holofernes. Young girls seem to have had a penchant for depicting decapitation. Other subjects include a king and queen, and allegorical versions of the five senses.

In addition to the central scene, these designs show seemingly unrelated animals, flowers, birds and insects jostling for position, with no attempt to maintain scale. Butterflies appear the same size as camels. Both flowers and animals are often drawn from the popular bestiaries and herbariums of the time.

All these subjects can be seen on the embroidered caskets of the second half of the 17th century. The ladies, some very young indeed, would embroider the silk panels, which were then professionally mounted as caskets. The finished casket was designed to show the needlewoman's skill and also used to store her precious jewels and cosmetics. Many of these caskets survive, although most are in less than perfect condition unless they were fortunate enough to have been stored in a custom-made wooden box, as was the case with the casket illustrated above left. Simpler versions are offered at auction several times a year.

In the Edwardian period (1901–10), 17th-century embroidery became popular, both for collecting and copying. Whilst these copies (known as "Revival embroideries") were never intended to deceive, they can pose a problem to the modern collector, as it is sometimes very difficult to tell the 17th-century example from the 20th-century copy. There is usually some difference in the colours of silks and in the quality of metal thread. It often pays to look at the faces, as it seems to be very difficult to keep a 20th-century expression at bay.

▲ Italian wall-hanging
Embroidered panels such as this would have hung on walls of castles and villas, c.1700.
£1,000–1,500/$1,600–2,400

# 17th-Century Continental Embroidery

Continental embroidery differs from its English counterpart quite markedly. Where English embroideries celebrate the intimacy of the close-up view, French and Italian equivalents are rather more sophisticated in subject matter, with Roman and Greek myths and legends the preferred choice.

The Catholic Church was also still a strong influence, and many ecclesiastical subjects also survive. The current market is rather unsympathetic to these pieces, keeping prices surprisingly low. In many cases, 17th-century embroideries of saints can be picked up quite inexpensively, and vestments are almost equally unpopular, unless they are of museum quality. You will also see altar frontals and orphreys (embroidered panels in the shape of a cross) from vestments quite frequently at auction.

Domestic continental embroideries can be divided into the urban and the rustic. Urban textiles for the wealthy tend to survive in some numbers as a result of their high quality, and of the fact that house

contents can remain untouched for centuries. High-quality silk, damask and velvet will all last better than their cheaper contemporaries. Rustic domestic embroideries are not common and have a limited following outside their country of origin.

In Italy and southern Europe, furnishing textiles are often of deep-piled velvet, especially crimson, and often feature gold thread embroidery and appliquéd scrolls and devices. A surprising number survive in excellent condition in the form of wall-hangings, sometimes with modern mounts. A study of Old Master paintings is useful in showing the richness of 17th-century Italian interiors.

The styles used in secular embroidered pictures tended to copy contemporary painting and print-making. Certain kinds of Italian embroideries are at first sight hard to distinguish from the print upon which they are based. Italians were also very fond of landscapes as a subject for embroidery. Many works copied prints or etchings exactly, and the quality is

**▲ Silk bed or table cover**
The red ground is embroidered in silver thread and
bears the monogram of the owner in the centre. Late
17th century, Italian. **£3,000–5,000/$4,800–8,000**

**► Table carpet**
Typical of the early 17th century, this piece is worked in
tent-stitched silks, with the ground restored in places. This
affects the value, but the carpet's rarity saw it realize a large
sum at auction. **£30,000–50,000/$48,000–80,000**

**▼ Embroidered carpet**
This large 17th-century embroidered carpet is worked in
flame stitch or Bargello. It was made in Hungary in the
Italian style. **£5,000–10,000/$8,000–16,000**

often extraordinarily fine. Being able to trace the
print on which a piece is based increases its value.
Embroideries inspired by the landscape around
Rome or major classical sites tend to be more
valuable than those inspired by unidentified
countryside. If this is your chosen area of interest, you
would be well advised to learn a little about contemporary prints and etchings and a little geography.

The French had an eye for Rococo detail. While
classical subjects are again preferred by most
collectors over secular embroideries, there can be no
mistaking the fact that the clothes worn in these pieces
are French and of the highest fashion, and that the
poses of the figures are elegant and contemporary. It
pays to have a knowledge of classical mythology.
When buying, you should bear in mind that prices in
France tend to be higher for native French embroideries. You should also bear in mind the value of
provenance to the continental market. Any link to an
aristocratic house or royalty will raise the price.

Stitches are numerous, but there was a marked
preference for *petit point* and *gros point*. These cross
stitches are usually on a loose mesh canvas. You
should be aware of 1920s copies of cross-stitched chair
covers and cushions, identifiable by the colours (copies
tend to include a strong pink) and by faces with
strongly delineated eyebrows and lips. Canvas from
the 1920s tends to be cotton rather than linen. The
faces of cross-stitched figures tend to wear faster than
their clothes, so beware of reworked faces.

Certain centres in France, such as Beauvais,
concentrated on embroidery where a fine chain stitch
was produced on hangings as well as costume. This is
also known as tambouring, after the French *tambour*,
referring to the large drum over which fabric was
stretched when being worked with a sharp hook.
The embroiderers of Beauvais, where the royal
factory was founded in 1664, continued to produce
chain stitch well into the 18th century, especially on
gentlemen's court costumes.

► **Virgin and Child by Mary Linwood**
An embroidered picture by one of the few named makers of the 18th century, showing her trademark imitation brushstrokes. Attributed pictures are extremely rare and highly prized.
**£4,000–8,000/ $6,400–12,800**

▲ **Ivory silk bedcover**
Typical piece with border of animals and birds, showing influence of Indian embroidery in the 1730s. **£2,000–4,000/$3,200–6,400**

◄ **Chair seat cover**
Embroidered with English flowers such as roses, irises and carnations, with the fashionable dark ground of the 1720s. Part of a set of chair seats and backs. **£500–600/$800–1,000** for single cover

# 18th-Century British Embroidery

British embroidery at the beginning of the 18th century was bold and colourful, and full of zest. In tandem with silk designs of the period, large full-blown flowers decorated embroidered seat covers, pictures and dresses. Costume and accessories were lavishly trimmed with embroidery at this time. Embroidered petticoats and aprons were popular for women, and embroidered waistcoats for gentlemen. Embroidered aprons are particularly inexpensive.

Early 18th-century interest in embellishing the domestic environment was particularly directed at chair and sofa coverings of canvas worked with tent-stitched silks or wools. Suites of embroidered seats and seat backs with a central urn of flowers, classical or pastoral scene in silks, framed with a darker-coloured border such as blue, rust or black are typical. The vignettes are often outlined in strapwork cartouches.

The scale of stitch is usually varied, with the smaller, finer stitch reserved for the central vignette and a larger, bolder stitch for the borders. The faces of central figures often wear thin and are therefore often restored. No matter how sensitive the restorer, it is usually obvious when this has occurred. Notions of beauty change with the centuries, so that a 1920s restorer may add something of the gamine to the 18th-century shepherdess, and a 1940s restorer may perhaps add a boldly painted mouth. Restoration of this kind reduces the commercial value considerably.

The dark-coloured outer borders received the most wear. Darker colours often used an iron mordant, which eventually corroded the silk or woollen thread. It is therefore common to find that the entire outer border has been restored and reworked. This was particularly popular in the 1920s and 1930s when mock-Tudor design and furniture enjoyed a resurgence of popularity. Restorers of this date often chose "old rose" for the outer borders. Reworked borders decrease the interest of the embroidery to collectors considerably. Unrestored suites of chair covers are particularly difficult to find

▶ **Embroidery in the style of Mary Linwood**
Because no documentation exists to definitely link this embroidery with Mary Linwood, the price is comparatively modest.
**£500–1,000/$800–1,600**

◀ **Lady's quilted waistcoat**
Another example of an Indian-influenced design. The ziggurats at the hem are a stylized version of the rocky mound of Indian tree of life embroideries. **£2,000–4,000/$3,200–6,400**

and expensive to buy, as the collector is in direct competition with the owner of period furniture.

Chinoiserie subjects vied for attention with the favourite floral subjects, and were treated with some charm, as were Indo-Persian motifs. These included the tree of life that was so common on Indian embroideries imported into Britain by the East India Company. Fashionable gentlemen in their libraries with their extensive collections of oriental literature often wore a loose gown, preferably of some exotic Indian chintz or "bizarre" silk. These robes were known by the Indian term *banyan*.

The second half of the 18th century was marked by the return of interest in classical motifs and mythology, and a renewed interest in naturalistic flower pictures. With this lighter style came a more flexible embroidery technique. Tamboured silks and linens appeared. It is sometimes very difficult to tell British tamboured embroidery from Indian as the designs were exchanged so regularly between India

and Britain. Occasionally, you will come across what on first glance appears to be a chintz, but on second glance turns out to be a chain-stitched embroidery. The chances are that this is in fact Indian, following a chintz pattern taken out to Gujarat in India for copying. Indian tamboured work often (but not always) features a dark green, almost dark blue outline, where British work does not. Many different articles were tamboured, from purses to waistcoats and bed curtains.

Towards the end of the century, embroidery began to take a less prominent role as fashions turn towards Grecian-inspired simplicity of design. Embroidered pictures became painstaking copies of contemporary prints, in coloured silks with details picked out in chenille thread. These print-based embroideries are also common in monochrome black silk or even human hair. A slightly mawkish sentiment is often detectable, which was mirrored in the interest in contemporary Gothic novels.

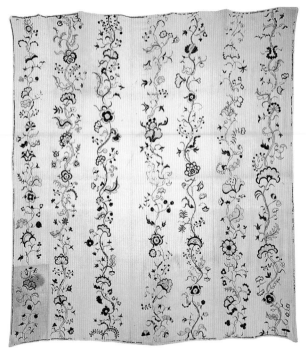

**▲ Crewelwork hanging**
This attractive hanging, worked in blue and white, is typical
of American crewelwork of the 18th century.
£8,000–10,000/$12,800–16,000

**▼ Letter wallet**
Embroidered in tent stitch. The dark ground and style of animals
and birds suggest that this is an 18th-century American piece.
£500–1,000/$800-1,600

# American Embroidery

The history of embroidery in America is very closely connected to that of Britain. By the 18th century, American society was well-established and social imitation, leading to the spread of fashions, was part of life. The economic control exerted by Britain meant that it was British luxury goods that were imported, rather than French, although French influence was paramount in Britain at the time. Therefore, in the first half of the 18th century, North America represented the largest market for English silks outside London.

As in contemporary Britain, domestic needlework was the mark of leisured refinement. In America this was emphasized by the fact that all imported luxuries remained expensive, including the raw materials that were needed to carry out embroidery, and only the wealthy could afford them. However, American embroidery also seems to have been partly stimulated by the scarcity of professional alternatives, and in the long-standing colonial tradition of homemade decorative textiles, practical items were generally made, including crewelwork, quilts, patchwork and canvas work for upholstery.

This led to the development of some distinct national characteristics by the mid-18th century, before the mass production and internationalism of the 19th century. Perhaps because of the scarcity and expense of materials, there is a spaciousness to the placing of motifs which gives an elegance to the overall design, as seen in surviving crewelwork and silk-embroidered examples. Blue is also a common colour, due to the production of indigo in southern America by the 1740s, leading to wide availability and low cost.

Canvas work was as popular in America as it was in Britain. Generally worked in wools, sometimes in silks, in tent stitch over a canvas ground, it was used for upholstery, screens and smaller items such as pocket books. It was popular throughout the 18th century and various subjects were worked, including pastoral scenes, often drawn up by local pattern-makers inspired by European engravings and illustrations. Florentine, or flame stitch, seems to have been especially popular. It was quick to work and no pattern drawing was required. The repeat could be simple or complicated, determined by the length of the stitching and the colour shading used. Pocket books,

► **Lady's pocket**
Designed to be worn under skirts, attached to the waist by strings. This example is particularly elaborate. The feltwork flowers point to an American origin.
£800–1,500/$1,300–2,400

▲ **Embroidered panel**
Of typically spacious design, with vine tendrils and natural-istic flowers.
£500–1000/$800–1,600

◄ **Appliqué feltwork picture**
The panel retains its original bright 18th-century colours.
£1,500–3,000/$2,400–4,800

in particular, were often signed and dated by their makers. Samplers were also worked, primarily as part of the education of a young girl, although by the mid-19th century there was a decline in teaching needlework as part of the school curriculum, partly due to the wide availability of printed cottons.

By the 1840s, the craze for Berlin woolwork (*see* pp.28–9) had reached American shores. This peaked in about 1856 but remained in fashion for the next thirty years, longer than in Britain. American examples of this kind of work are similar to their British counterparts, but some patterns, such as allegorical figures of America, were created specifically for the domestic market. Patterns were imported, and also published in American ladies' magazines. Most types of "fancy work" practised in Britain also found favour in America, with novelties such as braidwork being regularly introduced.

In 1876, the Royal School of Needlework exhibited at the Centennial Fair in Philadelphia. This attracted much interest, and led to the popularity of "Art Needlework" (*see* pp.26–7) in America. Similar insti-tutions to the Royal School were set up and proponents

of its style came to the fore. The American version of "Art Needlework" was influenced by the patterns of William Morris, and also by Japanese style, already familiar through the work of the American artist James Abbot McNeill Whistler. By the 1890s, a more distinct style had developed – for example, the use of silk threads instead of crewel wool and the rejection of the subdued tones of English pieces for fresher colours.

Connected to this was the establishment of the Deerfield Blue and White Industry, at Deerfield, Massachusetts, in 1896. The practice of early colonial blue and white crewelwork was successfully revived by the firm, although using linen threads in place of crewel wools. It was very popular until World War I and eventually closed in 1925.

The differences between American and British embroidery can be difficult to distinguish, leading to a scarcity of firm examples. However, where a piece can be determined as American in origin, notably with 18th-century examples, it is rare and highly desirable, especially to many American collectors, who are now realizing the value and strength of their own independent needlework traditions.

**▼ Altar frontal**
The central pierced Sacred Heart indicates this 18th-century piece, probably from Italy, was an altar frontal for an important chapel. £500–1,000/$800–1,600

**▲ Part of a wall-hanging**
The fine quality of this 18th-century piece, with the flower-encircled columns and typical full-blown flower-heads, makes it very collectable.
£15,000–20,000/$23,000–32,000

**▶ Pair of embroidered Italian slippers**
The couched metal embroidery on these slippers suggests an Italian provenance, 1720s.
£5,000–10,000/
$8,000–16,000

# 18th-Century Continental Embroidery

Continental embroidery of the 18th century is obviously not homogeneous and varies according to country of origin. Broadly, the major centres of production were France, Italy and the Iberian Peninsula. The trading and cultural links these countries held with the outside world affected their output. France was influenced heavily by classical civilization. Italy looked to the Ottoman Empire and beyond as well as to central Europe. Spain and Portugal had strong links with Arab culture in North Africa, and Portugal also had extensive colonial links to the Far East and India.

French silks were the finest in the world, and their embroidery was arguably equally fine both in furnishing textiles and on costumes. Embroidered coats and waistcoats were particularly successful, both for court dress and day wear. A relatively large number of embroidered suits from the last quarter of the century were preserved by families and appear regularly on the market.

Embroidered pictures and furnishings enjoyed a particular vogue at this time. Classical and pastoral scenes were preferred, with *gros point* and *petit point* the preferred medium. The quality of embroidered pictures of this time is very high, and they are becoming increasingly collectable.

Italy did not, of course, exist as a single state in the 18th century, so that defining general trends in embroidery can be difficult. However the Catholic Church was a very powerful influence and patron, and some of the best embroidery of the century was to be seen on vestments and altar furniture.

Domestic embroideries began to play a more important part in the interiors of wealthy and aristo-cratic Italian families. Predominantly on deep red damasks and velvets, their tone was sombre and rich, designed to look best in candlelight. Many of these survive and can be acquired relatively inexpensively although perfect examples reach high prices. The look of slightly faded grandeur is currently very popular.

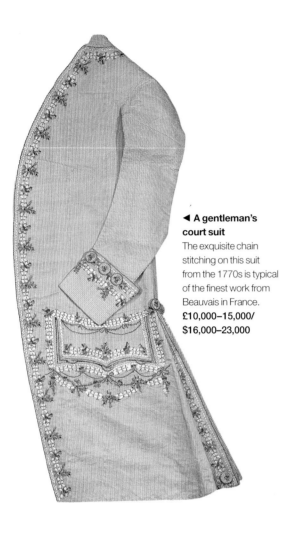

◀ **A gentleman's court suit**
The exquisite chain stitching on this suit from the 1770s is typical of the finest work from Beauvais in France.
£10,000–15,000/ $16,000–23,000

# Collecting Castelo Branco

▲ **Embroidered coverlet**
The beige silks used for the trunk of the tree of life – an Indian motif adopted by the factory – are characteristic of early 19th-century Castelo Branco embroidery.
£1,000–1,500/$1,600–2,400

The Portuguese were particularly prolific and accomplished embroiderers. Stylistically closely related to contemporary Italian works, the quality of embroidery is very high. Again, the Catholic Church remained the most important patron in the 18th century, but domestic embroidery was widespread, both as a folk art and in urban centres. Favourite combinations include ivory satin embroidered with designs of parrots, tulips and other flowers. It is sometimes difficult to tell whether an embroidery is Italian or Portuguese. A characteristic lime green can point towards Portugal rather than Italy, especially in combination with canary yellow.

At the moment, very little has been published on Spanish embroideries. This category has proved problematic in the past, especially in the early part of this century, when too many pieces were attributed to Spain in the absence of other evidence. One now has to be wary of Spanish attribution until further scholarship clears the present muddy waters.

A small factory run by nuns at Castelo Branco, in central Portugal, has become famous for the quality and quantity of its embroideries. This historic centre still produces embroideries to this day after original 17th-century patterns.

Generally, these embroideries take the form of bedcovers. The format usually includes a central medallion, either with figures, flowers or coats of arms. They are based on Indo-Portuguese embroideries from north-west India, particularly Goa, which was a very important Portuguese trading post.

Castelo Branco embroideries differ from their Indian counterparts in their use of large areas of flat, untwisted floss silks, loosely couched. The effect of this stitch is to allow long lengths of silk to catch the light, deepening the colours. The palette of colours is lighter than their Indian cousins, with a rose pink particularly characteristic.

Stylistically they tend to be more folkloric and naïve in drawing, whereas their Indian contemporaries are generally more sophisticated. Collectors can acquire 19th-century examples for relatively modest sums compared with Indian embroideries in the same style.

▲ **Appliqué panel**
The central motif of a
basket of flowers
suggests a German
influence or perhaps
German ancestors.
Early 19th century.
**£3,000–5,000/
$4,800–8,000**

▲ **Embroidered picture**
This superb picture, with its sophisticated figures, is signed and dated
1791. The black tent-stitched ground is a typical feature of the area
around Marblehead, near Boston. **£6,000–10,000/$9,600–16,000**

# American Appliqué and Needlework

The needlework tradition in America adopted a general approach of making the most out of a little. In the colonial period, this was partly because the raw materials needed to create such pieces were expensive luxuries and there was a scarcity of items, as well as a religious puritanism and a pioneering spirit, both of which continued well into the 19th century.

Appliqué was a technique much used in America, both in the 18th and 19th centuries. As well as being employed for quilts and patchwork coverlets, where it was generally cotton and chintz that was applied, elaborate pictures were also created using the same technique. Some of the boldest examples are ones where wool and felt-shaped panels have been applied to the ground, gradually built into the intended subject which was generally floral or pictorial. In the 18th century, wool was also an expensive import, so these pictures were created by affluent women who had

time to work on such intricate pieces, and are highly desirable to today's collectors.

Needlework pictures also performed a practical role in American society where there was little heritage in painting and printing by the mid-18th century. They were produced using European illustrations and engravings as their source. As with their European counterparts, popular subjects included allegories, floral arrangements, pastoral scenes and biblical subjects. They were often worked as a "graduation piece" by girls at an academy.

After 1810, there was a decline of embroidery as part of a girl's education, although mourning pictures with painted details were popular from 1800 and 1830. Slightly morbid to modern eyes, this style of needlework is sometimes known as Moravian embroidery, named after the sisters from this sect who taught it in the schools they had established in colonial America.

▼ **Appliqué bedcover**
Worked in the 19th century in a typically American technique which was also found in Germany in earlier times. £1,000–1,500/$1,600–2,400

◄ **Embroidered scene**
A late 18th-century pastoral design which includes a fine house and fashionably dressed lady and gentleman. £3,000–5,000/$4,800–8,000

Another specific type of American needlework was the bed rug, most surviving examples dating from the late 18th and early 19th centuries. They are often signed and dated, and were unique to New England and especially the Connecticut river valley.

Carpets were imported from the Orient via England and Holland during the 17th and first half of the 18th centuries, but were a luxury just for the wealthy. By the start of the 19th century, homemade rugs produced in a variety of ways begin to appear, their creation aided by the reduction in cost of raw materials as a result of industrialization.

Some embroidered rugs survive from the early 19th century, a few examples with squares of embroidery and appliqué stitched together to form the whole. The most elaborate have a combination of floral motifs, animals and human figures. Yarn-sewn rugs were another type, generally worked in the first half of the 19th century in a similar technique to bed rugs, using primarily wools and linen. They tend to be small, decorative pieces.

Hooked rugs are created from a related technique developed in America in around 1850, when burlap, an ideal base for hooking, first became widely available, instead of using a linen base. By the 1860s, the technique was widespread in the east of the country and by the late 19th century had spread across the whole nation. There are many designs and styles, as well as different shapes and sizes. By the 1860s, pre-drawn patterns were available, leading to a decline in original design but a more general uptake in the making of such rugs.

The thrift and ingenuity of the American needle-woman during the 18th and 19th centuries are evident in such pieces, which helps to make them highly collectable for those with an interest in America's past.

► **Bell pull**
This is a detail from an embroidered
bell pull made in the 1860s, used to
summon maid servants from below stairs.
**£100–200/$160–320**

# 19th-Century British Embroidery

One of the most popular embroidery techniques of the 19th century, plushwork is very closely related to Berlin woolwork (*see* pp.28–9). It became popular in the 1850s as a way of introducing a relief, or three-dimensional effect, into any canvas-work embroidery. It was worked using special plush wools in a loop stitch, also known as velvet stitch possibly because of the final texture produced. The loops were hooked through the canvas, held in place by cross stitches, then cut and brushed up before being clipped into contours as the design demanded.

This technique is usually seen in panels worked with exotic birds and flowers, the designs of which were taken from recently published coloured plates of books. These were most commonly from Edward Lear's *Illustrations of the Family of Psittacidae or Parrots* (1830–2), John Gould's *Birds of Australia* (1837–8 and 1840–8), and Audubon's *Birds of America* (1827–38), which contained over four hundred plates.

This effect was also known as tufting and could be produced by other methods. One was based on herringbone stitch, where row upon row was worked over a template, increasing in width until the area to be covered was completed. The stitches were then cut through the centre, the template preventing the canvas from being cut too, and the pile clipped to the required shape. There was also a more mechanical method which produced a fringe that could either be sewn on to canvas or used for a more free-standing three-dimensional effect. Specialist shops would trim plush to shape once it was in place on the canvas.

The expertise needed to carefully grade colours of wools to achieve an overall three-dimensional effect, as well as the precise final cutting and trimming of the piece, can readily be seen, and makes plushwork attractive to today's buyers. The subjects of the pictures also add to its appeal.

"Art Needlework" was the major movement in embroidery in the 1870s and 1880s. The Royal School of Needlework was founded in 1872, followed by similar institutions around Britain. The basic theory was to revive the art of embroidery through the thorough knowledge and study of historic examples, inspired partly by the revival in ecclesiastical

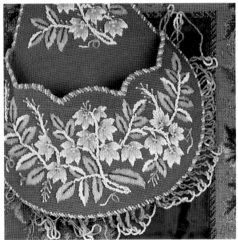

**▲ Embroidered pocket**
Made in the 1870s, this pocket was used to store hairpins and bows, and is embroidered with silk and trimmed with beads. **£50–100/$80–160**

**◀ Plushwork cockatoo**
A mid-19th-century plushwork picture of a cockatoo. The bird is of wool clipped to form a pile, and thus looks three-dimensional. **£500–600/$800–1,000**

needlework in the mid-19th century. By the mid-1870s, the craze for Art Needlework was as great as it had been for Berlin woolwork in the 1840s. Printed patterns were propagated through magazines and the stitches were generally simple, although the ideal was to design one's own pattern.

Sombre colours were generally used, perhaps in reaction to the harsh colours of Berlin woolwork. Its leading proponents were closely bound up with the Arts and Crafts movement, although it was practised across social classes, drawing its design influences from many sources. These included patterns influenced by Arab, Japanese, Moorish and Renaissance designs. Flowers such as sunflowers, irises, daffodils, daisies and narcissi were preferred. Likewise, cranes, herons and peacocks replaced parrots and birds of paradise. Such pieces were generally worked as covers, cloths, hangings, mats and piano covers rather than upholstery.

Other fashions include a craze for Anglo-Indian embroidery in the 1880s. This was worked on silk or wool furnishing brocades or damasks. The woven pattern was picked out with crewel stitch or stem stitch and then infilled with satin stitch, the centres worked with French knots. It was also worked on Indian cotton printed handkerchiefs that could be bought cheaply, and were often embellished with gold thread and sequins. A similar technique was applied with greater skill by the Leek Embroidery Society, founded in 1879 by Thomas Wardle at Leek in Staffordshire. Designs were worked on printed tussore silks, velveteen or cottons, and often have an Indian influence. If they can be attributed to the Society, these are highly collectable pieces today.

Many types of "fancy work", as contemporaries termed it, existed to enable the Victorian lady to pass her time, often with fads invented by manufacturers to promote their businesses. Examples include braidwork and ribbonwork, popular in the 1830s and revived in the 1880s under the name of "Rococo" embroidery. It is the larger pieces, such as curtains and hangings, which tend to be of the greatest value. By the 1890s, the influence of Art Nouveau and the Glasgow School of Art was felt and the nature of embroidery design changed once more.

# Berlin Woolwork

The term "Berlin woolwork" became virtually synonymous with embroidery during the 19th century, so widespread was the craze for such needlework. It is still easily found today, as unmounted panels, framed as pictures or covering everything from footstools to tea cosies. However, the quality does vary enormously and this is reflected in a wide differentiation in prices.

Berlin woolwork is canvas work, a type of embroidery that had been practised for several centuries and was commonly used for household furnishings such as wall-hangings and chair-covers. It was the privilege of the wealthy to undertake such work, which required both time and resources. In the 19th century, with industrialization, embroidery became generally an amateur occupation that was worked as a pastime rather than specifically to furnish the home or decorate costume.

In 1804 in Berlin, a printseller named Philipson published a pattern printed on squared paper, the colour design hand-painted in. A square of paper equalled a square of the canvas, so the pattern was easy for even an amateur to follow. In 1810, the publishing firm of L.W. Wittich, also in Berlin, followed the same idea, producing many more copies, also hand-painted. Their success in Germany was almost immediate and the rest of continental Europe followed.

In 1831, Wilks Warehouse, a major needlework shop in Regent Street, London, began importing large quantities of patterns and specially dyed German wool for working these patterns. To begin with, they were very expensive, so could be returned after use and part-exchanged for a new design. By the 1840s, the craze had taken off and mass-produced patterns were widely available both in Britain and America.

By 1840, there were around 14,000 different copperplate designs in circulation. The earlier pieces are generally on a small scale with delicate floral sprays, bouquets and similar repeating patterns. As patterns were mass-produced in the 1840s, they grew bolder in scale and colour and often reproduced pictures of popular artists of the time. Scenes from the novels of Sir Walter Scott were favourites, reflecting the current vogue for the Gothic and Medievalism, along with other historical scenes and ever-popular biblical subjects. Sir Edwin Landseer's animal studies were also used, particularly those of the royal pets, and these are still keenly sought after by collectors today.

Pieces were adapted to decorate every household object and some items of costume, including bell pulls, firescreens, cushions, slipper fronts and waistcoats. From the 1840s, beadwork was incorporated into the design, a bead replacing a stitch. The best beads were imported from France and, in some cases, beadwork

▲ **Berlin woolwork patterns**
These geometric patterns are typical of those used for rug borders or bell pulls. 1860s. **£40–50/$65–80**

▲ **Design for a pair of slippers**
Fathers were always the recipients of slippers for birthdays and Christmas. Those in the 19th century were hand-embroidered after patterns like this one from the 1860s. **£40–50/$65–80**

predominated with woolwork only used to fill in the ground or borders. Silk highlights were also introduced in the 1840s and 1850s, and these can be quite commonly seen in surviving examples.

In the late 1850s, the newly discovered aniline dyes produced bright new colours, often garish to our eyes. During the 1860s, the novelty of the aniline dyes made them highly fashionable and they were used in patterns reflecting the typical style of that decade, with large-scale naturalistic floral arrangements. The colours and designs were toned down by the 1870s, with a greater use of smaller-scale geometric patterns.

By the mid-19th century, Berlin woolwork patterns were cheaply reproduced and were included as pull-outs in the burgeoning women's magazine market. Titles such as *The Ladies' Treasury* and *The English Woman's Domestic Magazine* frequently featured patterns to cater for their middle-class readership who had newly acquired time on their hands to devote to such pastimes. They also offered advice on how to work them, although even for the novice needlewoman, the patterns and theory were both fairly simple.

The adverse side of these developments was that the patterns left little room for originality, with even the colours pre-determined. The two main stitches used were tent stitch and cross stitch. There was,

however, some variation in the canvas. The earlier pieces, pre-1840, generally have a canvas made of silk threads wound round a cotton core. The ground was often left unworked, exposing the canvas. Some of these Berlin canvases were also coloured, including shades of grey, pale purple, primrose and black. Later canvases, and the most popular, were made from cotton and produced in various gauges ranging from 4 to 15 threads per centimetre or 11 to 37 threads per inch. French linen canvas was considered the most accurate and evenly woven, and the later German cotton canvas the most helpful, as every tenth thread was coloured yellow.

The craze for Berlin woolwork began to decline during the 1870s, and in the 1880s was superseded by "Art Needlework" (*see* p.26–7). Since it was such a mass craze, much Berlin woolwork survives today across continental Europe, England and America. Pieces vary considerably in quality, and as patterns are not exclusive to a specific year, they can be difficult to date. One indicator is the colour of the wool, and whether it is a natural or aniline dye, another is the scale of the design. Some pictures sometimes have a date and maker's name worked into them. By looking at several pieces, one can soon distinguish a piece of quality against the more general work, which is still currently found in fairly large quantities.

# Samplers

## From the 17th to the 19th century: a young lady's accomplishment and a work of art

▲ **"Spot motif" sampler**
This type of sampler dispenses with the alphabet and concentrates on floral motifs and complex embroidery. It may been been used as a sample card by a professional needle-woman. Mid-17th century. **£1,500– 2,000/$2,400–3,200**

It seems from the physical evidence available to us today that young girls started to embroider samplers in the 17th century, although the need for a similar practice piece must have been present before this point. However, the sampler worked as a decorative and presentable picture seems only to have become widespread as one of a genteel girl's accomplishments in the 17th century.

Patterns were often taken from books of plant drawings and exotic animals, as well as pattern books. It is thought that itinerant sewing teachers were employed in large households. The style of samplers is, however, remarkably uniform, considering the range of young ladies who were obliged to complete one. Regional styles are in fact rare, and more identifiable on American pieces than British samplers.

The shape of 17th-century samplers is based on the shape of hand-woven linen. This is characteristically longer at the beginning of the century (typically up to 70cm or 27½in), and

shorter towards the end. Width varies but is on average around 20cm (8in) wide, becoming wider again at the end of the century.

The most interesting embroidered details are usually at the top of the sampler, with the owner's name and other information coming after the embroidered alphabet. Sometimes the top band is three-dimensional, with figures, flowers or trees. The more three-dimensional the work, the greater the value of the sampler.

Embroidery threads are generally silks, but wools also feature. Wool samplers are slightly less desirable commercially. Metal thread, that is to say silver and gold, is also used, especially in raised stitching. The presence of gold and silver will increase the price of a sampler, as only the élite would be able to afford this luxury.

One of the earliest types of sampler is the whitework sampler, which should perhaps be thought of as being both lace and embroidery. A long band of plain linen is embroidered in white, with bands of more or less elaborate

◀ **Commemorative sampler**
Sewn to commemorate an earthquake in London in 1692, the central panel is three-dimensional. **£5,000–8,000/ $8,000–12,800**

▶ **English or Scottish sampler**
Typical of the late 17th century, this sampler displays no raised work, but plays on variations of an undulating flowering vine. **£1,000–2,000/ $1,600–3,200**

openwork, which involves weft threads being pulled out to leave a transparent mesh of threads. Some will be worked with drawn threadwork patterns, where warp threads are bunched together with a stitch to form a pattern of holes. Some bands will be embroidered, some will have raised work. An alphabet sometimes features, but is not as standard as in coloured samplers. The best examples may have floral patterns or figures built up three-dimensionally using buttonhole stitch. The prices of such samplers rise with the quality of the embroidery and the inclusion of figures and raised work.

Coloured silk samplers tend to achieve the highest prices at auction, with raised work and the use of metal thread increasing the interest. Samplers with three-dimensional figures are the most sought after. American samplers will realize larger sums than British or continental samplers of similar quality because of their scarcity, and the larger demand in America for home-produced embroideries.

Any 17th-century sampler with an American provenance is by definition extremely rare and will attract enormous interest on the open market. This early in America's history there are very few stylistic differences between America and Britain, so one has to rely on internal evidence (in a signature) or provenance (family history). The value of a sampler, whether American or British, will be greatly enhanced if the text discusses a real event. Because samplers are so difficult to place in context, the collector should read the text very carefully for clues. For example, a sampler commemorating an earthquake in London in 1692 (illustrated above) is extremely unusual. Meteorological records confirm that this was no flight of fancy but a real event. At this point, the sampler becomes interesting not only to collectors of embroidery, but also to people interested in meteorology and the history of London. This is one of many examples of an embroidery revealing something about the history of the maker and of her environment.

**▲ Sampler by Caroline Brizley**
The stitching is simple but effective in this sampler by Caroline
Brizley, typical of the 1830s. £1,200–1,500/$2,000–2,400

**▲ Silk sampler, 1820s**
This sampler shows a sophisticated sense of design and was
probably worked by an older girl. £1,000–1,500/$1,600–2,400

**► Ship-motif sampler**
Probably continental, with unusual ship motifs and a very loose
structure. Dated 1762, initialled MEF. £1,000–2,000/$1,600–3,200

# 18th- and 19th-Century Samplers

By the 18th century, embroidering samplers was
firmly fixed as part of a young girl's education.
Sewing was a fitting occupation for a young lady and
enhanced her appeal on the marriage market.
Improving subjects were often chosen as the text of a
sampler. Indeed, some samplers in the form of tablets
of stone reproduce verses from the Bible.

Most improving texts, however, were intended to
remind the embroideress of the consequences of sin, in
much the same way that writing lines at school was
intended to reform the writer. A very stern verse with
few pictures is not only dull to embroider, but also to
collect – the prices of the more authoritarian samplers
are therefore usually far lower.

A nice compromise of improving subject with
artistic possibilities can be seen in the many samplers
showing Adam and Eve in the Garden of Eden,
placed either side of an apple tree around which the
serpent has coiled itself. Some collectors concentrate
on these samplers exclusively (*see* right).

The format of samplers in the 18th century
evolved from the long band sampler of the 17th
century to the portrait-shaped sampler of around 30 by
40cm (11¾ by 15¾in). The ground was still open linen
canvas and the threads were again silks and wool.
Metal thread was very rarely employed.

As in the 17th century, an alphabet generally
featured in the centre of the sampler. However, by the
1720s the rest of the space was increasingly taken up
by a scattering of decorative vignettes. Favourite
subjects included the maker's home, surrounded by
slips of animals and flowers. Samplers with large
pictures of houses, and especially named houses, are
extremely popular with collectors.

**▲ Sampler by Mary Harmer**
This portrait-shaped sampler dated 25 November 1802
is worked with the typical verses of a pious young girl.
The charming rabbits at the foot of the tree, along with the
figures of Adam and Eve at the top, help make this work
particularly attractive to collectors.
£1,500–2,000/$2,400–3,200

Exceptional subjects command exceptional prices.
One example featured an English redcoat soldier
impaling a kilted Highlander with his sword. It was
dated to 1747, the year following the Battle of
Culloden, and made ten times the price of a more
common subject.

In the 19th century, the size of the sampler itself
increased slightly. Alphabets still showed off the skill of
the stitching. Vignettes included homes, pets and
flowers. Homes featured in the centre, with naturalistic garden details. By the mid-19th century wool
became more common than silk as an embroidery
thread. The influence of Berlin woolwork (*see* pp.28–9)
became apparent by the 1860s with cross-stitched cats,
dogs and posies prevalent. The most elaborate of these
samplers frequently have the alphabet omitted, and are
very popular with collectors.

# Collecting
# *Adam & Eve Samplers*

**▲ Adam & Eve sampler**
A fine late 18th-century example of an Adam and Eve
sampler. The apple tree with its entwined serpent has Adam
and Eve standing on either side. Note also the profusion of
smaller vignettes, all adding to the considerable interest of
this embroidery. £1,500–2,500/$2,400–4,000

Focusing on the group of samplers that
features Adam and Eve at their centre would
be a particularly good choice for the novice
collector. They were mostly made in England
and Germany from the late 18th century until the
end of the 19th century. A good example would
include a tree with an entwined serpent in the
centre, with a more or less naked Adam and Eve
to either side. The treatment of the subject by
young girls ignorant of its charged nature can be
charmingly naïve or even on occasion coy. It is
nearly always dramatic. Verses tend to be rather
solemn, but the drawing of subsidiary motifs can
be charming. The depiction of Adam and Eve
can be stylized or highly elaborate.

As ever, collectors will want to get examples
from a range of representative dates, with as
many variations on the theme as possible.
Germans collectors seem to be particularly
fond of the Adam and Eve story.

Prices range considerably according to
quality, and it is often very difficult to predict
supply and demand in a collecting niche such as
this. The buyer will need to determine the value
of any one piece to his or her collection as a whole.

◄ **Sampler by Martha Southwood, Dublin, America, 1836**
Simple but charming, this sampler has the assets of name, date and town to increase its value to a collector.
£500–800/$800–1,500

► **American sampler**
An unusual example, signed and dated with a portrait of a lady and gentleman in the margins.
£1,500–2,000/ $2,400–3,200

◄ **Mourning picture**
This kind of embroidered picture appears in several variations. The American provenance of this one, dated 1795, will increase the value considerably. £1,500–3,000/$2,400–4,800

# American and School Samplers

Most samplers give limited information about the embroideress. The usual details might include the sewer's name, age and the date, with occasional mentions of place or the name of her house. The details are very similar to those you would find on a gravestone. Anyone who has spent any time looking at churchyards knows how much one would like to know what the deceased died of, what their profession was and what role in society their family might have played. Curiosity is a very strong human impulse as is the desire to be able to set things in context.

The same frustrations apply to the sampler collector as to the graveyard historian. Occasionally, two samplers by the same girl turn up together allowing one to assess her progress. This is usually the limit to the wider picture gained from the data on a typical sampler. When you find a sampler with more information, even as little as a picture of the maker's house, the collector becomes more interested. When the county or state is given along with the girl's name,

the sampler becomes a part of history. The prices for such pieces will rise accordingly.

One of the groups which command interest in this respect are the so-called "School Samplers". While most samplers were worked at home with the guidance of a governess or itinerant teacher, some appear to have been worked under more systematic supervision. The teacher's name or the name of the school features on the sampler, usually in the same place on each sampler.

One such teacher in England was Judith Hayle. She seems to have been active very early in the history of samplers, in the 17th century. Her pupils appear to have been very well taught, as the surviving samplers are of high quality. Very little is known about her but her initials, IH, appear on a number of good-quality embroideries alongside the initials of the girl who embroidered the sampler. The style of embroidery is consistent in these pieces, tending towards finely worked geometric pattern and detail. Several of these

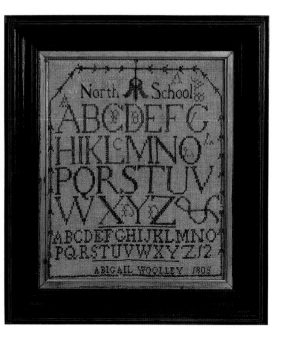

◄ **North School sampler, by Abigail Woolley, 1805**
The school provenance will increase the value to a collector even
though the sampler itself is rather modest, as befits its Quaker origins.
£1,000–1,500/$1,600–2,400

► **American sampler**
An accomplished sampler by Hannah Maxwell
of Philadelphia with neat drawing and good
design, dated 1827. The colours may have
faded slightly from their original state.
£3,000–5,000/$4,800–8,000

pieces are held by important institutions in both the
United Kingdom and America.

Judith Hayle's counterpart in America was the
Quaker Elizabeth Marsh, whose family came to
Philadelphia from England in 1723. She was soon
teaching children of the city's most prominent
families, and, with her daughter Ann, produced fine
work which always arouses much interest in the
saleroom. One of Ann Marsh's samplers – a supreme
example within a recognizable group worked
between 1723 and 1740 – was sold for just under a
quarter of a million dollars in New York at the
beginning of 2000. In a field where information is in
such short supply, a documented piece such as a
school sampler is worth a great deal to collectors.

School samplers continued to appear during the
19th century. Instead of the refined drawing of the
17th- and 18th-century schools, they concentrated on
dramatic pictures, perhaps a detailed picture of the
school building with its gardens, in which every

window pane will be lovingly depicted. They too
have a strong following among collectors.

At the end of the 19th century, there was a revival
in the production of school samplers. Public schools
began to take over the education of young ladies in a
more formal manner – each pupil produced a band
book on matriculation. This would include cotton
pages starting with workday darns and inserted
patches, and finishing with a miniature wardrobe
comprising nightshirt, knitted stockings, mittens and
underwear. Sometimes the pages of the book are a
continuous folded band of cotton, sometimes a metre
(39½in) or more in length. The purpose of these books
was to demonstrate that the maker was capable of
clothing herself and her future family.

If you find one of these books in its original state,
you will be very fortunate, as they have often been
looted by doll owners and collectors. However, they
remain one of the most charming and sought-after
records of a young girl's sewing education.

► **Sampler by Rachel Hook**
An unusual example by Rachel Hook dated 1805,
showing her home, the surrounding lakes and a
particularly stubborn-looking horse.
£2,000–4,000/$3,200–6,400

◄ **Dutch sampler**
Almost monochrome with tiny spot motifs. The top
row is typical of continental work in presenting the
initials of the entire family tree. Dutch samplers, unlike
German ones, are often square in shape – this is dated
1820, with initials WS. £500–1,000/$800–1,500

# European and Colonial Samplers

British and American young ladies seem to have been the most prolific embroideresses, if their surviving output is reliable evidence. However, by the end of the 18th century, European and colonial samplers began to rival British samplers in quality, if not in quantity. In Europe, the greatest number of samplers came from Germany and Holland, and during the 18th and 19th centuries they both produced work of the finest quality. Whereas British girls were being encouraged to add pictures to their alphabets, their European counterparts seem to have been encouraged to embellish the alphabet itself, leading to substantial contrasts in style.

The difference in subject matter is reflected in the shape of continental samplers. With the emphasis on the script, the band of linen can be longer and narrower than is usually found in England or America. In fact, a 19th-century German sampler is closer in shape to a 17th-century English band sampler rather than contemporary English samplers. Concentrating on the script also tended to lead to a narrow colour range, usually monochrome red, to show off the calligraphy and stitching against the white ground.

In the mid-19th century, however, continental embroideresses began to add small vignettes of animals and figures to their work. These miniature pictures are extremely detailed and can include eight or ten pictures in a single sampler, showing dogs, cats and birds as well as love tokens, hearts, crowns and other symbols. English samplers very rarely commemorate events, but continental samplers frequently celebrated important family events such as marriages – the bridal pair's initials and love tokens usually flank a minute embroidered portrait of the two figures in wedding costume, often with the priest officiating at the ceremony. Such samplers form part of a wider continental tradition of marriage tokens that includes painted chests and furniture, commemorative pottery, embroidered waistcoats and treen, amongst other folk arts.

One tradition of sampler embroidery to note is that of Mexico's colonial population, which produced superb samplers, worked by well-to-do ladies, from the 18th century onwards. They are in the European style, featuring elegant ladies in 18th-century, or even 17th-century-style costumes that were no longer worn in Europe but continued to form part of a fashionable

**▲ The African Slave, Esther Stewart, 1836**
Several variations on this anti-slavery image, popular with collectors, are known. £500–1,000/$800–1,600

**▶ Dutch sampler**
A small but perfectly worked sampler, with windmills, signed AG, 1821. £1,500–2,000/ $2,400–3,200

# Collecting
# *Darning Samplers*

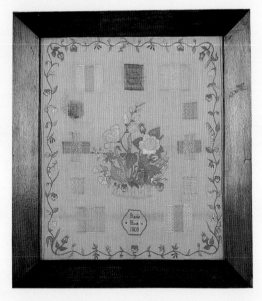

**▲ Darning sampler by Rachel Hook, 1803**
In this early 19th-century work, Rachel Hook has succeeded in turning humble darns into attractive decoration. £400–600/$640–1,000

lady's dress in Mexican colonial circles. The figures are typically clad in striped and flowered open robes, with turbans, lace caps or elaborate coiffures. The complexion of the ladies is often relatively dark compared to European samplers and the script is usually in Spanish. Mexican samplers of the 18th century are usually larger than American or English contemporaries, and a landscape format is favoured. The silks are generally untwisted, and slightly softer and thicker, and also more pastel in tone than those used by English and American embroideresses. The quality can be very high indeed.

One of the charms of samplers is the diversity of their sources: European missionary movements often encouraged embroidery alongside religious education, and their schools in India, for example, produced finely-worked samplers, predominantly in monochrome red silks in the Tamil language.

In the 19th century, European samplers tend to become monochrome, with the emphasis on neatness and fine stitching rather than on the sampler as an attractive picture. The exception to this trend is, of course, Berlin woolwork (*see* pp.28–9), which revelled in colourful vignettes of animals and flowers.

Making a darning sampler was a practical way of getting a young girl to practise invisible mending. This was a skill much in demand and which she would have used throughout her life. Once a needlewoman had acquired a certain level of skill, she began to think about forming the darns into decorative patterns and using silks of a contrasting colour to the ground. A favourite method was to work a tree trunk with leaves of ghostly cross-motifs. Sometimes alone, or in combination with a floral vignette, the finest examples were pretty enough to display alongside other samplers.

The price of these samplers is determined by the fineness of the stitching and by an early date. Most seem to date from the late 18th to the early 19th centuries, and are usually English. Darning samplers are not the kind of embroidery that appeals to a novice collector. On first inspection a darning sampler has a very discreet appeal – there are no pictures to recommend them immediately to the untrained eye. However, I would strongly recommend new collectors to take a closer look at the workmanship, as darning samplers are a taste well worth acquiring.

# Purses & Reticules

## From the 17th century on: exquisite collector's items for keepsakes or for coins

▲ **The Penn Purse**
Depicting Admiral Sir William Penn (father of the founder of Pennsylvania), his famous dog and a globe symbolizing his journey – the link to the Founding Fathers makes it almost priceless. Sold in 1983 for **£55,000/$88,000**

Purses in the 17th century were not primarily designed to hold money. The most elaborately embroidered examples were often sweetmeat purses or letter wallets. Both letters and sweetmeats were precious commodities and were kept in suitably precious envelopes – it is rare to find these purses with their original documents. Purses of this period are most commonly square in format and typically around 8cm (3in) square. They are embroidered on both sides and suspended on a decorative braided drawstring. Each corner of the purse, and sometimes also the centre of each side, has an elaborate tassel, as do the braided drawstrings. These tassels are usually composed of a large wooden bead wrapped in silk threads with a metal or silk fringe. They are easily damaged and lost so should be carefully checked – a missing tassel can be expensive to replace.

The care and attention lavished on the embroidery on these purses can result in work of outstanding quality. Many of the best examples have metal ground, with the silk design standing out against silver. The stitches are sometimes flat, in counted stitch or split stitch, but are often three-dimensional.

There are also many beadwork purses from the second half of the 17th century, sharing the same vocabulary and styles . They can look surprisingly fresh as beads do not fade with time. However, the threads on which they are strung can be fragile and should be checked. Only a single thread is used, so any damage can unravel large areas very quickly, and repairs are expensive.

The Tudor rose is a popular subject, as are symbols of love and sentiment, such as the gillyflower, with its curative properties and sweet smell. Given the lack of hygiene (and indeed dentistry), prose, poetry and embroidery

**▲ Flame-stitched wallet**
An 18th-century American wallet, used for keeping important letters. This pattern, which takes its name from the resemblance of the stepped blocks of vertical stitches to flames, is also known as Florentine stitch or Bargello. **£400–800/$640–1,300**

**▼ Work bag, dated 1669**
Embroidered in red silks with unusually fine spot motifs, these kinds of bags contained needlework in progress, along with tools.
**£1,000–2,000/$1,600–3,200**

in the 17th century revelled in all sweet smells. Scented flowers such as honeysuckle, which had the added pictorial virtue of entwining itself around its support, are therefore extremely common on embroidered purses. Sugar was an expensive commodity, but highly valued, and both sweet peas and strawberries were also worked on love tokens. Plays on words such as "deer" and "dear", and "hart" and "heart", resulted in many leaping stags, often pierced by love's dart or by Cupid's arrow.

Woven purses from this period are equally elaborate. Most are woven from silks, with metal thread details. The most bizarre to modern eyes, however, are those woven of human hair, brocaded with gold thread. To the untrained eye, these purses might seem to be brown silk. Opinion is generally divided equally into those collectors who find this thread appealing and those who find it appalling. The use of hair as a

raw material is not uncommon in jewellery – there is an obvious correlation with hair jewellery of the Victorian era, for example. By definition, this kind of weaving is rare and commands considerable interest at auction.

Other purses to look out for include gentlemen's gaming purses, which are circular pouches, usually but not exclusively of rich red velvet, gathered by a drawstring. The flat bottom of the purse is often embroidered with the owner's crest or coat of arms. The circular shape is designed to sit perfectly at the corner of a card table, holding gaming tokens or coins. Many of those surviving appear to be French in origin.

By the end of the 17th century, the square double-sided purse had made way for flat, embroidered envelope purses or reticules closed by a drawstring. Embroidery becomes more important on the wallets, usually in patterns closely related to woven silk patterns.

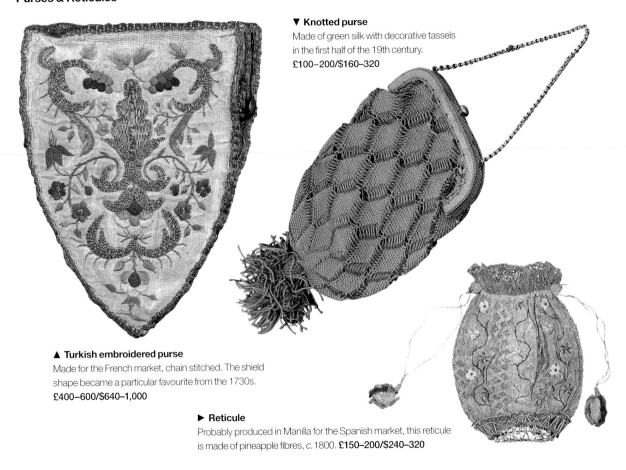

**▼ Knotted purse**
Made of green silk with decorative tassels
in the first half of the 19th century.
**£100–200/$160–320**

**▲ Turkish embroidered purse**
Made for the French market, chain stitched. The shield
shape became a particular favourite from the 1730s.
**£400–600/$640–1,000**

**► Reticule**
Probably produced in Manilla for the Spanish market, this reticule
is made of pineapple fibres, c. 1800. **£150–200/$240–320**

# 18th-Century Wallets and Drawstring Purses

The 18th century saw a dramatic increase in the variety of shapes and sizes used for embroidered purses and wallets. These were still kept in pockets suspended from a belt around the waist, with access to the more voluminous tear-shaped pockets achieved through side slits in the lady's petticoat. These pockets were produced in pairs, and although they were not on public view, considerable time and energy went into their decoration. They remained a vital place for carrying necessities – a lady would otherwise only carry her fan and a decorative handkerchief, and, by the end of the century, a drawstring reticule suspended from her wrist.

Silk wallets were still a staple on the fashionable young lady's dressing table. They held letters and keepsakes, and could themselves be presents from admirers. Many are worked with hearts and flowers or other lover's tokens. They can, however, also commemorate a loved one. These mourning wallets are usually embroidered in sombre black silk or hair on white satin. They commonly show a tomb on which the name of the departed is embroidered, with a weeping maiden kneeling alongside. Those which are embroidered with human hair are especially collectable – a quick glance might not reveal that the black thread on the purse is actually hair, so taking a magnifying glass when purchasing is recommended. Larger silk envelopes also began to be produced during the 18th century, sometimes quilted and embroidered, but sometimes plain. Embroidered wallets were a convenient method of filing documents.

Novelty shapes for purses became a feature. Shield-shaped purses became fashionable in the middle of the century. This shape required a metal frame to open and shut the purse, rather than a draw-string. Motifs tend to be of fruiting vines and flowers, and such purses are generally bound in gilt braid, stiff in the hand rather than flexible.

**◄ Document wallet**
A rare English wallet from
c.1750–75, made of ivory
linen, quilted and embroidered – such pieces are
popular with many collectors.
**£500–1,000/$800–1,600**

**▼ "Miser's Purse"**
So-called because coins were only extracted
with difficulty. Made of silk and cut steel
beads, this early 19th-century example is
unusual in having the name, Samuel
Stockford, worked into the purse ends.
**£100–200/$160–320**

**► Beaded bag**
This evening bag, worked with
medieval-style portrait heads,
would have been purchased rather
than made at home. Dated 1902.
**£100–200/$160–320**

From the 1780s and 90s, fashions changed and heavy silk and wool dresses, which were open at the front and worn over petticoats, were replaced by less formal high-waisted dresses, known to us from the paintings of Thomas Gainsborough. These dresses were made of light, floating silks and muslins. With the change in silhouette came a change in the purse or pocket. A bulky pair of pockets would have been visible and would also have interrupted the line of the dress. Access to pockets hung from the waist was difficult in these flimsy dresses so the pocket was therefore abandoned in favour of drawstring purses or reticules.

A reticule hung from the wrist by a thin braid. The fabric of these purses was as light and fluid as the dress silks and therefore they were often made of transparent mesh or net, whether embroidered, knotted or woven. They were not intended to hold anything bulkier than a silk handkerchief. The lady would also carry her fan suspended from the wrist.

Gentlemen also used wallets and work envelopes for important papers. In fact, leather wallets became a fashionable gentleman's accessory for the man about town, as they were usually a sign that he had been abroad. When young men set off for southern Europe on the customary Grand Tour of the classical sites, they not only brought back sculptures and paintings but also decorative document and letter wallets. Many were, in fact, expensive souvenirs of travel. Ottoman and Moroccan leather wallets are indeed often embroidered in gilt thread with the traveller's name, the date and the place of production.

They seem to have been produced in Istanbul primarily, but also in North Africa, particularly in the city of Tetuan. They continued to be produced throughout the Ottoman Empire from the late 17th to the 19th century. Many collectors search out these wallets and are particularly interested in those with uncommon names or places.

**▼ Three net purses**
In the 1820s, young ladies were required to produce such purses to carry their dance cards and a handkerchief. The lower bag is more capacious and may have been intended for needlework.
£150–200/$240–320 each

**▲ Three cross-stitched purses**
These colourful geometric patterns are typical of the 1850s, and were almost certainly homemade.
£40–60/$70–100 each

# 19th-Century Embroidered Purses

The variety and quality of purses and reticules in the early part of the 19th century are a delight to the collector. The first decades of the century saw fashions moving away from the elegant whites of neo-classical drapery towards vibrant colour, especially canary yellow, aubergine and mint green, which were all new dyes at the time. With the move into colour came a change in shape as well, towards a fuller, rounded sleeve and a love of frills, so long suppressed.

This affected the shape and form of accessories, too. The start of the century saw slim, knotted or embroidered silk purses. By the 1830s the shape had filled out to a figure-of-eight, rounded shape, often flat, often embroidered with exuberant sprays of flowers. The purses were designed to lie flat, showing all the pattern at once, and were not intended to carry anything more bulky than a handkerchief, fan and dance card.

Aerophane purses were a particularly charming speciality of the 1830s. Taking ribbons of a transparent silk gauze, which were pleated, folded and appliquéd on to ivory silk, ladies created charming purses and reticules to take to balls and parties. To the modern eye, the flowers look as if they were made from stockingette. If you are particularly lucky, you might find work-baskets trimmed and made up entirely of these flowers.

The most common shape of purse in the first half of the century was the miser's purse, a long, narrow tube of knotted silk with a slit halfway down. Coins were kept in either end of the tubular purse by two rings pushed down at the ends. Few of these survive in good condition, firstly because of their construction and secondly because the decorative rings and tassels were often recycled when the purse wore out. Prices for these purses are still very attractive.

The middle of the 19th century saw a resurgence of knitted purses, especially beaded purses produced primarily in Germany. These were often produced as souvenirs and are often worked with the word *Andenken* ("souvenir" in German). Babies' bonnets in

**▼ Evening reticule**
This silk reticule has a beadwork trim. The chenille tassels are typical of the 1830s and 40s.
£100–120/$160–190

# Collecting 20th-Century Handbags

**▲ Hermès bag**
This clutch bag made from glossy black crocodile leather is a typical Hermès piece of the 1930s. **£300–500/$480–800**

the same technique are also collectable. The size of the purse has become smaller and designed to fit inside a more voluminous "handbag". These outdoor bags began to be made in leather, cloth or even in carpet plush. A "carpetbagger" was originally a traveller.

By the 1870s, flat bags suspended on cords often matched a lady's outfit. The braids and ribbons were often extraordinarily elaborate. This was also the decade when cut-steel beads again became popular. These beads tend to rust if not kept dry, at which point their commercial value plummets. This decade also saw a craze for Turkish tapestry woven bags, often with matching slippers. They were produced in Turkey in great numbers both for export and internal use, when the Turkish upper classes adopted Western dress.

Collecting these purses offers something to satisfy most tastes and budgets. Whether your preference is for the elegance of the early 19th century or for the exuberance of the 1880s, there should be a purse which will charm you.

The 20th century offers some interesting handbags to the collector. There are many handworked bags of great charm, from 1900 to World War I, which remain relatively inexpensive. The beaded evening bags of the 1920s can also be picked up for modest sums. Their quality is usually high and design interesting, especially in the mid-1920s when Art Deco and Cubist designs began to be translated into wearable pieces.

Elsa Schiaparelli, the muse and friend of the Surrealists, dared to team impeccable tailoring with outrageous accessories. In collaboration with Salvador Dali, she designed one of her most famous handbags in the shape of a telephone, with a scarlet lobster as the receiver.

The 1940s and 1950s saw the rise of Hermès, who still produce the famous triangular "Kelly" bag, from a commission for Grace Kelly. The original models are now highly priced, and other Hermès models, with the characteristic H-shaped buckle, will be much less expensive.

An enduring name to conjure with is that of Paco Rabanne, whose aluminium and chain-linked bags have retained their 1960s appeal. Biba and Mary Quant are other "swinging" labels for collectors to look out for.

# Beadwork

## From the 17th to the 19th century: a durable and attractive craft in which the freshness of the colours is preserved

A very common reaction when faced with 17th-century beadwork is to doubt that it can be old at all. Because it is so strong and durable, many pieces survive in almost mint condition, unfaded and fresh. A look at the reverse of the picture or at the thread should be reassuring, and forgeries are at present rare.

Both the French and Italians produced high-quality beadwork, usually for furnishings such as wall-panels or hangings. A characteristic of Italian beadwork found on altar frontals is the use of opaque tubular white glass beads as the background for embroidered silk flowers, along with a sacred heart or the initials AM for "Ave Maria". Beadwork pictures with these cut-glass tubular beads can also appear on the market, while some grand Italian houses have entire rooms hung in beadwork landscapes of this kind.

Because such tubular beads have sharp, cut edges, the silk around them has often been damaged over time, leaving a tangle of threads and loose beads. Restoration of this work is time-consuming and costly, assuming that a restorer can even match the beads. Condition is therefore very important when considering whether to make purchases. Beadwork birds, for example, were generally made from larger-scale beads so can look deceptively youthful and vigorous, but any damage to the underlying wire structure will be extremely expensive to restore without dismantling large areas – a 17th-century example in sound condition is thus highly sought after.

Although continental beadwork dominates the early 17th century, English beadwork is unmatched in the second half of the century, reaching a high point in the 1660s when smaller, rounder beads became available due to technical advances in the glass industry, allowing more detailed work. Needlewomen were therefore able to produce more complex pictures and expand their subject matter and vocabulary.

The most common beaded items that the collector can still discover are beaded purses. Produced for the wealthy, these purses show a high degree of sophistication. They are generally flat, with tassels at each corner and closed by a decorative drawstring. Subject matter is very similar to contemporary embroidered purses,

◄ **Beadwork basket**
Seen from above: a beadwork basket of the 1660s with naturalistic berries, fruits and flowers. Baskets such as these were used at an infant's christening.
£4,000–6,000/$6,400–9,600

► **Beadwork picture**
A sovereign receiving his queen in a tented pavilion is depicted in this well-preserved work from the 1660s.
£2,500–3,500/$4,000–5,600

◄ **Beadwork picture**
This picture from the 1660s is similar in style to contemporary embroidered pictures. It shows a couple surrounded by emblems of the British Isles. In original tortoiseshell frame.
£1,500–2,000/ $2,400–3,200

and includes endless knots symbolizing eternal love, or deer and arrows, or the flowers associated with the language of love. Beadwork lends itself very successfully to inscriptions. Many purses have the owner's name, allowing them to be dated. Any such details will increase the interest to collectors. Colours tend to be slightly more sombre than those of embroidered purses, with brown beads particularly popular as the ground, and opaque blue, white and yellow beads picking out the patterns.

Beadwork is also used for other accessories, such as decorative knife handles and needle cases, and also occasionally for three-dimensional objects such as sprays of flowers. Rare novelty beadwork needle cases can be in the form of frogs and other small animals. Collectors should be aware of catalogues of needlework such as the Irwin Untermyer Collection. Many such collections were dispersed in the interwar years. Examples of beadwork which can be cross-referenced with these catalogues are very attractive to collectors. Their rarity and the relatively small number of serious collectors means that they are often traceable in literature.

Three-dimensional English beadwork was also used to great effect on the beadwork baskets used to hold the infant's clothes and bearing cloth during the christening ceremony. They generally have raised openwork sides, about 6cm (2¼in) deep. These sides are sometimes composed of a lattice, and sometimes of three-dimensional sprigs of flowers. The floor of the tray often incorporates the infant's name and the date of birth. The base and outside of the basket will also be finished in beadwork.

The best beadwork is most often seen in beaded pictures of the 1660s. Here, the ground is usually of opaque white beads. It seems that these pictures were intended to be beaded versions of contemporary embroidered raised-work pictures, as they differ only in that one is embroidered, the other beaded. Because beadwork does not fade, they can show the collector what the original colours of embroidery might have been like in 1660. They are eagerly collected, as they represent a high point in the history of beadwork which is probably only exceeded by French *sablé* or sand beadwork of the following century.

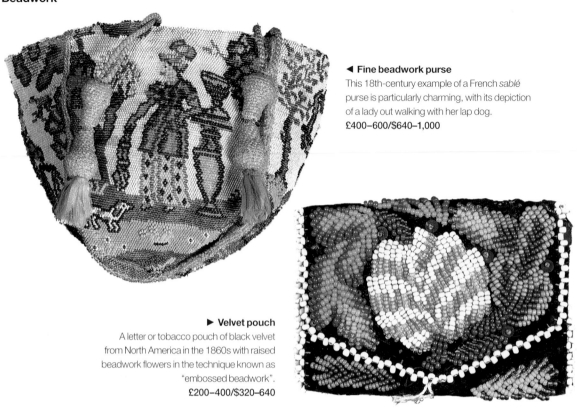

# French and North American Beadwork

In the 18th century, French beadwork was by far the best in Europe. Very fine glass beads were newly available in clear, dense colours, allowing delicate features to be worked into the patterns. The finest French beadwork is known as *sablé* because the beads resembled grains of sand (*sable* in French).

This type of beadwork is found on a diverse number of objects, mainly on a small scale. The most common objects are probably needle cases. These gilt metal tubular cases were oversewn with a beadwork net, typically a sky blue or white ground scattered with flowers. Small vignettes of pastoral scenes were also popular, often featuring shepherdesses and their lovers. Knife and fork handles were another common object as beads are obviously durable and clean so are ideally suited to this purpose. Sets of knives with beadwork handles will appeal not only to textile collectors, but also to collectors of 18th-century porcelain, and thus can reach high prices. Scent bottles can also be charmingly beaded – again the language of love is used to decorate these pieces, and can include mottoes and cryptic love tokens.

The height of the art was, however, used to create beadwork drawstring purses. French embroiderers were able to give full reign to their imagination. Quivers of Cupid's arrows, hearts and flowers abound. These purses are usually lined in fine plain-coloured silk or damask. If you are very fortunate, you might find a lady's beaded garter of the late 18th century, usually a gift to the bride, which can occasionally be worked with a slightly saucy *double entendre*. The return gift to the bridegroom was often a set of beaded braces with white kid fastenings.

Equally charming are shoes of the 1780s and 90s. Mules and ladies' slippers are sometimes completely worked in *sablé* beads. These slippers were intended for the most fashionable – usually only one pair appears at auction every year to an eager reception. Beadwork of the highest quality continued to be produced in France throughout the 18th century, but by the 19th century it was virtually indistinguishable from beadwork in Germany, where beadwork bags were produced in the 1840s and 1850s similar in style if not in quality to French *sablé* purses of the 18th century.

A white beadwork piece with entwined initials and the inscription "Ici est mon secret" (Here is my secret), suggesting it may have contained love letters.
£500–1,000/$800–1,600

**▼ Tlingit buckskin moccasins**
The colour of these moccasins of the inland Tlingit people suggests a date around 1900.
£2,000–4,000/$3,200–6,400

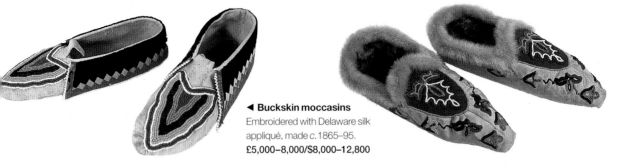

**◄ Buckskin moccasins**
Embroidered with Delaware silk appliqué, made c. 1865–95.
£5,000–8,000/$8,000–12,800

In the 19th century glass beads were introduced to the native cultures of North America by European traders. Prior to this date, beads used for ceremonial purposes and as a means of barter and exchange had been made by hand from seashells. They were generally white, with a lesser number of purple beads, and were known as wampum. The first trading in beads began when a group of fishermen landed in Newfoundland and Prince Edward Island and set up their permanent camp. Trading involved the exchange of iron nails, axes, jewellery and porcelain for pelts.

These transactions continued successfully until the question of territory arose. The displacement of tribes into neighbouring territories and eventually into reserves clearly had an effect on the textile traditions of the native peoples. However, the introduction of glass beads effectively replaced the use of quill embroidery and shell beads completely. In fact, the availability of these beads proved a creative spur and instigated new patterns and formats into the native vocabulary. These were clearly native in origin and were not European patterns grafted on to the native culture.

The first beads imported were called "pony beads" because they arrived on the traders' ponies, and were applied to various items by two basic methods. The first is known as "spot stitch", in which a string of beads is tacked to the ground at short intervals. Curves and arabesques are therefore possible. The second is known as "lazy stitch", in which beads are threaded on to a needle and tacked down with the same thread, only really allowing beads to be applied in straight lines. In the 1860s, lazy stitch was used in combination with padding to produce "embossed beading".

The Great Lakes tribes were divided by technique. The northern groups, such as the Ojibwa, used infilling parallel to outlining beadwork, facilitating shading. The southern groups, such as the Potawatomi, filled in straight, parallel lines, not following the beadwork outline. South-eastern tribes tended to produce naturalistic floral schemes with white beads predominating. The Plains peoples produced geometric designs in lazy stitch over extensive areas in patterns associated with quillwork. In the 1870s, these patterns were influenced by the oriental rugs imported by European settlers.

**▼ Beaded purse**
This design of a tomb with a flame of remembrance in a garden is typical of German work of the 1840s.
£150–300/$240–480

**▲ Firescreen**
Fixed to a pole stand, these were designed to shade a lady's face from the heat of the fire. Here, typical Berlin woolwork patterns of the mid-19th century have been used.
£500–800/$800–1,300

# 19th-Century Beadwork

The British became especially enthusiastic about beadwork in the 1840s. The fashion continued right through to the 1870s and 80s. Beads are obviously durable, cleanable and attractive. They were therefore used to decorate a diverse number of objects and fabrics.

In the mid-19th century, beadwork was still a decorative trim principally used in borders and fringes. Purses often had a beadwork fringe, for example. It was at this time that jet became popular on mourning costume. Bodices, bags and skirts could all be trimmed with jet fringing, which was usually jet glass rather than a semi-precious stone. The fashion culminated in the many tiered capes and mantles of the third quarter of the 19th century. The sheer quantity of jet-trimmed costume available has kept prices very low indeed, and costume can therefore be acquired inexpensively. In an age when a large proportion of the population was obliged to wear mourning at any one time, decorative alternatives to black crêpe were very welcome. Even 19th-century beadwork can still unravel dramatically, so the collector should be careful to avoid damaged pieces as restoration can prove time-consuming and expensive.

More attractive to collectors are the beadwork bell pulls used to summon maid servants from below stairs. These can be up to 2 metres (6ft 7in) long, and always feature a design which is vertical rather than horizontal, usually a climbing stem, often convolvulus or bell flower. Tea cosies and tea trays also appear with beadwork panels. Even small pieces of furniture such as nursing chairs, pric-dieu prayer stools and footstools were worked with beadwork upholstery. Hassocks for use in church were also popular. All these pieces of furniture need a hard-wearing upholstery.

◀ **Beaded velvet panel**
Cut-steel beads and silks
decorate this late 19th-century
velvet panel for a wedding
celebration, from Singapore.
£400–600/$640–1,000

◀ **Chinese gilt purse**
Decorated with repoussé work,
Singapore, 19th century. The reverse
is velvet with beadwork flowers.
£400–600/$640–1,000

▶ **Evening bag**
A lady's beaded evening bag, in
the manner of Berlin woolwork
of the mid-19th century.
£200–500/$320–800

Most 19th-century British beadwork echoes the original colours of contemporary embroideries and the patterns used for Berlin woolwork. However, grisaille beadwork, worked entirely in grey and white beads, became very popular in the 1870s. The grey beads used on subjects such as cherubs and classical nymphs and statues are worked to suggest three dimensions or low relief.

Other European countries do not seem to have taken up beadwork as enthusiastically as England. There are, however, beadwork traditions which are very collectable, from countries as far afield as Singapore and India. Singapore has a long tradition of beadwork embroidery on velvet. The bride and bridegroom's wedding costumes are often elaborately beaded. The bride's slippers would usually have beadwork fronts, and both groom and bride carry

triangular velvet panels with beadwork borders which represent a ceremonial 'kerchief. Free-standing beadwork panels worked with birds and flowers also form part of the ceremony, as do beaded belts and pillbox hats. Often the beadwork alternates with repoussé gilt panels.

Kathiawar in north-western India also produces attractive beadwork that quite often appears on the market. The most common objects are door surrounds and friezes worked with angular camels and figures in brightly coloured beads against a white ground. Almost any textile can be beaded, even masks for sacred cows. Beadwork squares worked with a grid pattern were originally game boards (*chaklas*). Examples from the 20th century can be picked up at very low cost as most people remain unaware of the origins of such pieces.

# Silks

## From the 14th century on: the precious fabrics epitomizing luxury that travelled along the Silk Road

▲ **Chinese embroidered cover**
Worked on a ground of Imperial yellow silk, this embroidered cover was probably part of a set of daybed covers with matching cushions made in the 19th century during the Qing dynasty.
£1,000–2,000/$1,600–3,200

Silk production needs a warm dry climate and a plentiful supply of mulberry leaves for the voracious silkworms. It also needs a skilled work-force to process the raw cocoons and spin the silk. The first stage of the production process sees the moth cocoons boiled in a large cauldron. A hooked stick is then used to draw up individual threads and to wind them on to the stick. The threads need to be degummed in order to become supple. In its natural state prior to washing, this silk is often known as *tussah* silk or slub silk.

The knowledge of the method of producing silk was a closely guarded secret of the East. The Chinese exported the finished silks to Europe along the caravan road that leads from China, through Central Asia and Turkey to southern Europe. All along this road are cities built on the trade passing through their gates.

It is not known for certain when the first silkworms were brought to Europe. Legend has it that silk first came to Europe in the 14th century in the sleeves of a monk who had been given the cocoons as a gift. He smuggled them out of China to Europe. Whatever the truth of this story, acquiring silkworms meant that the West was able to produce its own silk and was not entirely dependent on China for imports along the Silk Road. Chinese weaving technology was still far in advance of Europe, and woven silk continued to be imported as a luxury item even as late as the 18th century.

All silk exports from China passed along the Silk Road, using camel caravans to cross the inhospitable plains and mountain ranges. Alongside the raw material, aspects of Chinese culture passed along the same route, with motifs such as the cloud band and lotus buds spreading to Sassanian Persia, Turkey and India.

▼ **Cantonese bedcover**
Made in the Portuguese colony of Macao by Cantonese craftsmen around 1800, this bedcover is embroidered with exotic birds, and was probably intended for export to the lucrative European market.
£2,000–4,000/$3,200–6,400

▲ **Japanese wall-hanging**
The entire ground of this distinctive19th-century piece is covered with cord-couched decorative whorls, as is the knot of phoenix. £5,000–6,000/$4,800–9,600

In China itself, silk gauzes were produced for home consumption alone, which displayed a degree of technical achievement that was unknown in medieval Europe. The exciting excavations of early tombs in China in recent years have opened our eyes to the sophistication of these weavings. Mummies which are clothed in the finest brocades and in patterned silk gauzes, trimmed with tapestry-woven bands, have been discovered, rewriting the existing history of silk-weaving.

Patterned gauzes seem to have been a Chinese invention, whereas tapestry-woven techniques seem to have come to China via Central Asia. The Mongols under Ghengis Khan displaced populations from Central Asia and set them down in China. A tribe known as the Uigurs, for instance, was renowned for its tapestry-woven silks. The displacement of this population may explain the appearance of the technique in China. It is found from the early Han dynasty (AD 206–220) to the early 19th century, and is known as *Kesi* (formerly known as *k'ossu*). Today it is the most sought-after technique among collectors, examples from the 11th and 12th centuries only appearing on the Western market in the last twenty years via Tibet. It is mainly available through specialist dealers but is making appearances at auction too.

Textiles from later dynasties are available in some quantities , thanks to merchants and missionaries of the 19th and 20th centuries who brought back large quantities of costume from their tours of duty. As a result of the Cultural Revolution in 20th-century China, which required the destruction of "decadent" Imperial textiles, China is not a major source for Chinese textiles. More pieces are now available in the West – the flow along the Silk Road is now, therefore, reversed.

**▲ Fifth civil rank badge**
Depicting a silver pheasant of the fifth rank, *c.* 1900.
**£200–400/$320–640** for a pair

**▲ Third military rank badge**
The third rank leopard. The straight
lines of the seawave border indicate
a mid-19th century date, as does
the profusion of cloud bands.
**£500–1,000/$800–1,600** for a pair

**► First civil rank badge**
With a crane, woven in *kesi*
(tapestry) technique in the mid-
19th century. The green ground is
made from peacock-feather
filaments. **£1,000–2,000/
$1,600–3,200** for a pair

# Chinese Rank Badges

Chinese rank badges are a popular area of collecting, both in Europe and the United States. The subject is one which is quite well documented, so offers a good range of possible avenues to explore. Most collectors will try to assemble a complete set of these badges, which are about 15–20cm (6–8in) square. Once this is achieved, the collector will then be interested in acquiring the best possible examples available, either by word of mouth, or in auction rooms. A certain number are now appearing on internet sites.

The badges reflect the structured nature of the Chinese court, which was rigidly prescribed by Imperial edict. It was run by an intellectual and largely, though not exclusively, aristocratic civil service, who either won their place at court through sitting a series of examinations, or bought an academic title and thus a position. This system relied on a mandarin's rank being immediately visible. To this end, he was required to wear a hat with a finial denoting his rank and a badge on his outer coat.

Every item of a mandarin's costume at court was prescribed in the *Huangdchoa liqui tushi* or "Catalogue of Ritual Paraphernalia" of 1766. For the most formal occasions, a *chaofu* robe with pleated skirts was required, and for less formal occasions, a *chifu*, also known as a "dragon robe". The robe's colour was laid down. Blue was the Qing dynasty's characteristic colour, replacing the red of the Ming dynasty. Yellow was the Imperial colour, with apricot and brown considered shades of yellow. Over the *chifu* was worn the *pufu*, a dark blue plain silk coat, on which the wearer's rank badge was applied or embroidered. The front badge was split either side of the opening. The back badge was uncut.

As the wearing of the outer surcoat was only required after 1759, most badges are from the 18th and 19th centuries. Earlier badges certainly exist and are much coveted. However, before this point, the symbol of rank was embroidered or woven directly into the court robe. Fewer have therefore survived.

**◄ First civil rank badge**
Depicting a crane; the outer border of this
18th-century badge is a later addition.
**£2,000–4,000/$3,200–6,400** for a pair

**▼ Pair of fifth military rank badges**
These late 19th-century military rank badges
are embroidered with a bear of the fifth rank.
**£300–500/$480–800**

**► A pair of ninth civil rank badges**
Woven in *kesi* (tapestry) technique, this badge
depicts a ninth-rank paradise flycatcher.
**£400–600/$640–1,000**

The Imperial family had a separate system of rank badges. They were allowed to wear roundels with the five-clawed dragon. The highest ranking members had a front-facing dragon, while the lesser members had a side-facing dragon. The Qianlong emperor (1736–1795) added the Imperial symbols to his roundels on the *pufu* coat. He added the sun (cockerel) and moon (hare) symbols to each shoulder and *shou* characters to the front and back roundels. These symbols also appear on Imperial robes, with 12 symbols being retained for the Emperor. Towards the end of the 19th century, hoofed dragons appear for lower-ranked noblemen.

If you find a badge with a simple bird or animal seemingly floating in a cloud-filled sky, you may well have a badge from 1898. In this year the Emperor instituted a reform period known as "The 100 Days of Reform". All the peripheral sea-wave borders and auspicious symbols were removed. These badges have a great appeal and are collected as rarities. Badges with

pairs of leopards or cranes may well be Korean and could be several times more valuable than a comparable Chinese badge, as the Korean court was much smaller and fewer badges were produced.

Rank badges can be embroidered, brocaded or tapestry-woven (*kesi*). Of the three techniques the latter is the most sought after. Generally, the quality of these badges is higher than their equivalent in brocade. The weavers began to incorporate peacock-feather filaments into the weave, which also increases the value of the badge considerably.

Dating the badges is difficult but some general rules include the fact that the later a badge is, the smaller it tends to be. Towards the end of the 17th century, a sun disc often appears, symbolizing the emperor. The bird or animal is always looking at the sun. Stylistically, the badges tend to fill with symbols in the 19th century, whereas earlier badges are simpler and barer. Colours deteriorate with the introduction of chemical dyes in the mid-19th century.

▼ **Safavid dynasty coat**
The silk of this coat is woven with a
cloth of silver ground with marigolds.
£5,000–10,000/$8,000–16,000

◄ **Cloth of silver panel**
This piece, approximately 20 by 40cm (8 by 16in)
is brocaded with delicate flowers, and dates from
the late 16th or early 17th century.
£1,000–2,000/$1,600–3,200

► **Safavid dynasty panel**
An unusual silk panel of c.1700,
1.5 by 1m (58½ by 39½ in),
woven with crickets and butterflies of Chinese inspiration.
£2,000–4,000/$3,200–6,400

# Persian Silks

Iran, formerly Persia, lies on the ancient silk route
between China and the Mediterranean and so has
always been involved in the trading of silk.

When Shah Abbas I (1588–1629) conquered the
region, he sought to centralize its production into one
industry under royal control. The activities and
revenues of the industry played a major role in
cementing the infrastructure of his empire. Trading in
silk was discouraged until it had been shipped to
Isphahan, the capital, where merchants were then
permitted to buy and ship bales.

In the 17th century, production centered on Yazd,
Kashan and Isphahan. The cost of gold and silver in
luxury silks meant that weavers were financed either
by the Shah or by merchants. Subsidiary industries
such as dyeing were all subcontracted by the state at
fixed tariffs. Although European companies were on
hand, they found a more flexible and cheaper trading
partner in India. Persian luxury goods were therefore
chiefly for internal consumption.

The design vocabulary of Persian art is based on an
adherence to Koranic rules which prohibit the
depiction of the human figure. The majority of
designs are therefore based on flowers and elaborate
arabesques. This is not to say that pictorial silks do not
exist. Indeed, some of the finest 16th-century velvets
and silks feature courtiers and dancers. However,
these are the exception rather than the rule.

Of the Persian silks available in surprising
numbers today, brocade fragments from the 17th and
18th centuries predominate. One can only suppose
that the intrinsic value of the gold and silver thread
protected them from negligence. These silks were
usually designed for costumes and commonly feature
delicate flower sprays arranged in orderly rows
against cloth of gold or silver grounds. A number of
17th- and 18th-century brocades of this type were
made up into the short jackets made popular by the
later Qajar court (*see* right). It is therefore common to
find a 19th-century jacket made of 17th-century silk.

**▲ Safavid dynasty brocade**
This silk brocade square is woven with the large-scale
flowering shrubs that are typical of the late 16th century.
The piece is about 40cm (16in) square.
£300–400/$480–640

# Identifying Qajar homages

**▲ 19th-century homage to Safavid dynasty silk**
Many such versions of 16th-century silks were woven in
the 19th century in admiration of the earlier textiles.
£200–300/$320–500

Persian silks from the 19th century show a marked
change of emphasis from restrained to exuberant.
Strong colours and abundant gilt thread characterize
the silks of the later 19th century. Striped, satin-faced
satins known as *atlas* were popular for kaftans.

Dating these costume silks is made easier by
examining the size of individual motifs, which tend to
decrease from flower sprays around 10cm (4in) high in
the late 16th century to small, floral buds of only 1cm
(⅜in) by the 18th and early 19th centuries. In the 17th
century, selvedges tend to be less than 5cm (2in) wide
and striped, whereas 19th-century selvedges tend to be
reinforced with cotton and wider.

A general rule as far as value is concerned is that
the more complicated the design, and the more gold
and silver is used in the weaving, the more expensive
the silk becomes. Some of the most charming silks
feature deer and other animals sheltering beneath a
flowering shrub. This astonishing level of technical
accomplishment has arguably never been surpassed.

The Qajar Empire (1779–1924) looked
back in admiration to the court of Shah
Abbas I. As a result, many Safavid motifs were
reworked in the 18th and 19th centuries, and
Qajar versions of earlier silks pose problems
to today's collector.

The piece illustrated above is a Qajar
version of a Safavid silk. The survival in such
depth of colour of the particularly thick, black
outline of the figure points towards a later
date. One expects black silk to be more
corroded because of the iron mordant used in
its dyeing. In effect, black dyes rust. Experience
will point out the slight angularity of drawing
as will the feel of the piece in the hand. Qajar
silks tend to be rather thick and inflexible,
where a Safavid silk moves more fluidly.

There is no substitute for experience in
handling and examining these pieces: the
short viewing periods in auction rooms often
provide the best opportunity for this.

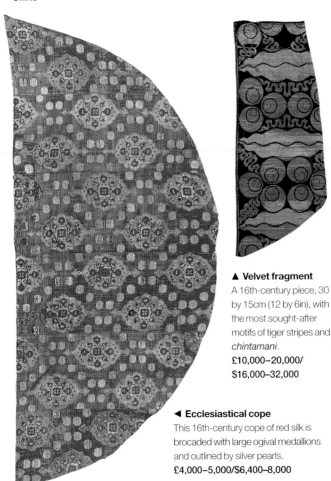

▲ **Velvet fragment**
A 16th-century piece, 30 by 15cm (12 by 6in), with the most sought-after motifs of tiger stripes and *chintamani*.
£10,000–20,000/ $16,000–32,000

◀ **Ecclesiastical cope**
This 16th-century cope of red silk is brocaded with large ogival medallions and outlined by silver pearls.
£4,000–5,000/$6,400–8,000

▲ **Fragment of silk lampas**
A museum-quality 17th-century silk, probably intended as a kaftan silk.
£8,000–10,000/$12,800–16,000

# 16th- and 17th-Century Ottoman Silks

The Ottoman Empire was long-lived and extensive, built on the foundation of the Byzantine Empire and stretching from its capital, Constantinople, to North Africa. A high point of patronage of the arts was reached when Suleiman the Magnificent reigned as Sultan from 1520 to 1566.

Contemporary reports of the court always described the magnificence of the textiles, from cushions and wall-hangings to robes of state. In fact, decrees in 1574 restricted the use of cloth with gold and silver thread to the Imperial workshops at the Topkapi Palace in Istanbul, so that the finest velvets, silks and brocades were not available on the open market. Miniature paintings of the day are very good dictionaries of style, as each robe is depicted in the smallest detail.

Only a few of these court textiles filtered out through a complicated system of honorific gifts, where official guests such as ambassadors would be presented with fine kaftans of sumptuous silks and brocades. Today, sultans' robes from the whole of the Ottoman Empire can be seen in the Topkapi Palace. Fortunately, they were preserved and tagged there, each one wrapped individually as they were immensely valuable. This ordered state of affairs survived until the end of the 19th century, when the stores were reorganized, and robes removed from their labelled wrappers. Some did not return to their original documented wrapping, so that this potentially unique inventory is, sadly, not a straightforward record. In addition to the Topkapi collection, several early 17th-century children's kaftans of Imperial quality have come to us through the tradition of draping the Prophet Mohammed's tomb with precious textiles. Some of these are now in the Victoria & Albert Museum, London.

The workshop system encouraged considerable cross-fertilization of ideas, so that an Iznik tile, an embroidery and a book cover might all use the same design vocabulary. The most popular motifs were the tulip, the carnation, the tiger stripe, the three pearls of

► **Bolster cover**
This 17th-century embroidered *yastik* (bolster cover) shows a well-known pattern of large tulips and palmettes. £3,000–5,000/$4,800–8,000

▼ **Silk panel**
A typical 17th-century silk, with pomegranates, tulips and roses, 80 by 150cm (31 by 59in). £8,000–12,000/$12,800–19,200

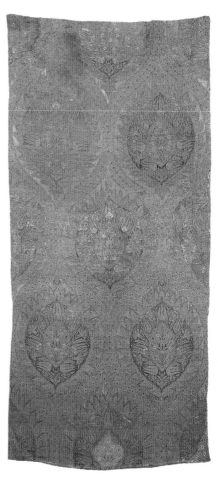

► **Large silk panel**
17th century, in a worn condition. £2,000–4,000/ $3,200–6,400

the *chintamani* design, and the pomegranate. Where all these are united in one design, the price will rise accordingly. Collectors have a particular fondness for the combination of tiger stripe and *chintamani*.

At the height of the 16th century, the size of design repeats is very large, sometimes over 60cm (23¾in) in length. The effect is extremely dramatic. Obviously more work has to go into designing one large motif rather than into repeating smaller patterns. The size of these motifs tends to get smaller as the 16th century progresses, until, by the end of the 17th century, they begin to form small sprig motifs rather than bold edge-to-edge designs.

Techniques of the 16th and 17th centuries include fabulous brocades, figured silks and velvets, with the use of metal thread perfectly mastered. Embroideries were also produced throughout the Ottoman Empire. Embroidered textiles from its outer reaches produced designs with a regional slant. For example, Epirus and Yannina in the Greek mainland produced

Ottoman designs which nonetheless call on local traditional styles. The same is true of Algeria, Morocco and Tunisia.

Embroideries take the form of bed covers, cushion (*yastik*) covers, diaphanous muslin wrapping cloths and turban covers. Large covers are usually formed by several lengths of hand-woven linen and then embroidered over the seams. Unfortunately, over the centuries, these larger pieces tend to have been split up, so that discovering a whole coverlet is an exciting find.

Woven textiles survive in lengths, or as fragments. Robes from the 16th and 17th centuries are now museum pieces, but fragments of 17th-century silks are relatively common and not necessarily expensive.

The market for complete Ottoman textiles of the 16th and 17th centuries in good condition is very strong. As the supply diminishes, the demand increases for good pieces. Damage or alteration severely depresses the value of these textiles more than most, as the home market is not enthusiastic about restoration.

◄ **Turban cover**
This 18th-century
turban cover has a
very fine muslin ground
and silk embroidery.
The blue flowers show
a Greek influence.
£2,000–4,000/
$3,200–6,400

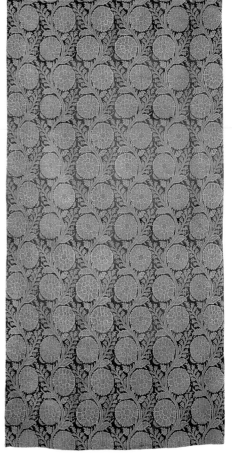

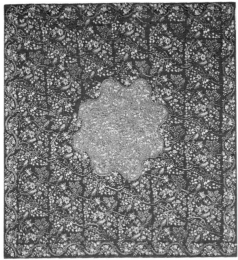

► **Embroidered
cover**
This 18th-century
cover, or *bocha*, is
of a red Kashmir
wool which would
have been
imported along
the Silk Road.
£500–1,000/
$800–1,300

▲ **Silk brocade**
A length of silk brocade with
undulating ribbons of flowers
typical of the late 17th century.
£4,000–5,000/$6,400–8,000

# 18th-Century Ottoman Silks

By the reign of Ahmed III (1703–30) the Ottoman Empire was established and passing from conquest to stable rule. Textiles of the time reflect this. The designs become more stylized and smaller, with delicate undulating floral ribbons. The outsize, bold designs of the previous century were no longer required, and refinement was the keynote. By the end of the century, the empire was still powerful but losing impetus. The textiles of this date were following a similar pattern.

The emphasis was in fact changing from court to domestic: expensive gold and silver and velvets made way for lightweight silk and brocades, and most characteristically for diaphanous gauzes and embroidered muslins. The main clients for expensive textiles were no longer the vizirs and courtiers, but their womenfolk. Although still in the harem, they had a very important commercial influence.

The move to the domestic arena also meant a shift away from brocades towards embroideries. Most surviving 18th-century textiles are in fact embroideries. Technically, the linen ground is stronger than 18th-century silks, so that this may be coincidence rather than a historical fact. However, the likelihood is that more pieces were produced either at home or by commercial makers for the home.

The most common fabric for these embroideries was fine, handwoven gauze, although a lightweight silk, commonly pale blue or yellow, was also used. Stitches on muslin are various, and on silk are usually chain stitches, made with a tambour hook.

▼ **Embroidered cover**
Probably made for a bed or quilt, this linen cover of the late 17th century has silk embroidered palmettes and flowers.
£20,000–25,000/$32,000–40,000

▲ **Embroidered cover**
A linen cover of c. 1700 embroidered in silks – note the Ottoman tulips and carnations.
£20,000–30,000/$32,000–48,000

The pieces that survive today are more likely to be domestic items, such as the covers that were used to protect a gentleman's turban while he was not wearing it, the embroidered squares known as *bochas* and the long sashes known to most in the West as towels, which wrapped up a lady's clothes while at the Turkish baths (*hammam*).

The baths were an important forum for social intercourse for women, as they represented the only occasion on which ladies left the confines of the harem. It was the place where marriages were agreed and weddings planned. When a young girl and her mother went to the baths, therefore, they would exhibit their finest embroideries, many of which have survived and can be acquired at relatively small expense.

Robes from the 18th century, especially ladies' robes, can still be found. They take the form of an open kaftan, cut tightly to the waist, with scalloped edges and long, open scalloped sleeves. They are nearly always striped, either of brocade or embroidered. The diaphanous under-robes can also be discovered occasionally, although by their nature they tend not to survive in any number.

The sashes which held up the voluminous trousers worn underneath such robes are also very collectable. Generally of fine cotton or of linen, they are usually worked with a decorative floral end-panel. Sometimes this panel also shows pagodas and townscapes. The more unusual and fine the embroidery, the more interesting and valuable it is to collectors.

**▲ Ottoman prayer mat**
The velvet ground and the landscape design
distinguish these 19th-century Ottoman
appliqués from those of Rescht in Iran.
£800–1,500/$1,300–2,400

**▼ Mosque curtain**
Composed of various coloured satins, all embroidered with inscriptions
from the Koran. This 19th-century mosque curtain is in excellent condition,
whereas the majority have suffered wear or damage.
£3,000–5,000/$4,800–8,000

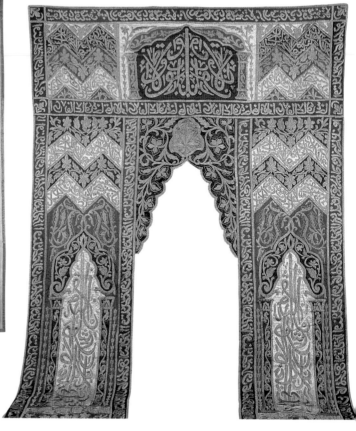

# 19th-Century Ottoman Silks

As the Ottoman Empire began to lose power in the 19th century, its design vocabulary became more stylized. Mainland Turkey, however, continued to produce textiles of high quality, although the emphasis moved from expensive court silks to more domestic products. There was no longer the same demand for expensive furnishing textiles, although *yastiks* (bolster covers) in the 16th-century style, with tulips, carnations and *chintamani*, were still produced in large numbers. The quality, however, had changed for the worse with the introduction of harsh chemical dyes and of silks of cheaper qualities.

Mosque curtains in the shape of *portières* survive in some numbers. Generally composed of panels of satins and velvets of various colours, embroidered in couched gilt thread with calligraphic medallions and arabesques, they can be spectacular. Most originate from the second half of the 19th century.

Further religious needs were met by prayer mats. Usually with a velvet ground, which shows underneath the *mehrab* or prayer arch, they often incorporate an appliquéd wool townscape or a large urn of flowers. These are extremely popular with collectors. Assuming that the velvet ground is still intact, they can make good sums at auction.

In the 1870s the Turkish court adopted European dress, with far-reaching effects on Turkish design. European elements creep into traditional patterns. A ribbon tied in a bow is almost universal at the end of the century. However, because it had been copied from a foreign design, many Turkish designers had not understood what they were drawing. The result is bows which are stylized to the point of abstraction.

Not only the design vocabulary but also the types of embroidered item changed. Prior to this time, a bride would have commissioned or embroidered her

◀ **Prayer arch**
An 19th-century example in burgundy satin, embroidered in couched gilt threads with an arch and mosque lamp.
£400–500/$640–800

▲ **Velvet cover**
A red velvet cover dating from the 1870s, embroidered in couched gilt threads, which would have been used as a table or tray cover for offering wedding guests coffee and other hospitality at the wedding ceremony.
£300–400/$480–640

trousseau herself. In the 1870s the wedding trousseau became Europeanized and would generally include a set of bed-furnishings of a pastel silk embroidered in gilt thread with flowers and foliage, owing much to French silk design of the time, which was made by professional seamstresses.

Occasionally of silk, but more commonly of velvet, *yastiks* were a staple of the textile trade. Originally produced in Bursa, the traditional centre of the velvet industry, by the 19th century the town of Scutari was mass-producing velvets in the same format: two narrow bands at either end composed of lappets, each with a motif, usually floral.

In the 16th century motifs such as tulips and carnations fill the field with one dramatic image. This motif gets progressively smaller until, by the 19th century, it is replaced with floral sprays. The width of the velvet increases from about 50cm (19in) to nearer 64cm (25in).

Today's collector will usually find the selvedge of a 19th-century *yastik* to be crumbling as they are loosely woven. The selvedge contains thick cotton strands to strengthen it and is usually about 1cm (⅜in) wide. A 16th-century selvedge is narrower, usually shot with a green stripe and tightly woven. Early *yastiks* are now rare and command high prices.

Weavers of the 19th century were not able to reproduce the colours of 16th-century velvets using their cheaper-quality silks and dyes. A 16th-century crimson is deep and jewel-like, with slight variations in colour. In the 19th century, weavers tried to reproduce this *abrash* (cloudiness) by weaving in irregular shaded stripes. However, you can always see when this is mechanical rather than a natural effect of vegetable dyes. With experience, you will be able to feel that the pile of a 19th-century velvet is never as deep as that of an earlier velvet.

◀ **Silk border**
A 17th-century Italian border woven
with *trompe l'oeil* silk fringes.
£500–800/$800–1,300

▲ **Silk panel**
A fine red silk woven with pomegranates,
made in Italy in the 16th century.
£700–1,000/$1,200–1,600

◀ **Lampas**
This 16th-century silk lampas is of
superb quality from Spain, and is
woven with hunting animals.
£4,000–5,000/$6,400–8,000

# Early European Silks

The cultivation of silkworms, the spinning of the cocoons and the weaving of silk threads was established both in Spain and Italy as early as the Middle Ages, although silk thread was also imported from the East. A lively exchange of woven textiles along trade routes also existed, with places as far afield as the Middle East and India. This may explain the links in terms of design between Asian and European silks during the Renaissance.

Production probably began in Sicily, placed as it was on the trade route between Asia, Europe and Africa. As early as the 12th century, Sicilian weavers were producing silks for royal commissions which bridged Islamic and Christian traditions. However, production was limited to the weaving of tapestry borders in the manner of weaving of the Egyptian

dynasties. By the 13th and 14th centuries, the main industry was situated in the states of the north of Italy, firstly in Lucca, followed by Venice. For the next four hundred years, Italy was to be the foremost producer of silks and velvets.

The weaving techniques of these silks are various. Italian velvets were world-famous both for their quality and design. Silk damasks reached a zenith of technical excellence. A more complicated weave, the silk lampas, was used for expensive silks. It was complicated to work, but stabilized metal thread well.

For the textile collector, ecclesiastical vestments can be superb finds, as the Church recycled precious silks, velvets and embroideries over the centuries. A 19th-century chasuble may well have an orphrey composed of 15th-century Italian velvet or damask.

▲ **Silk panel**
A large panel of red silk made in southern Europe (probably in Italy) in the 17th century, woven with an ogival lattice with urns of tulips, carnations and other flowers.
**£1,000–2,000/$1,600–3,200**

# Identifying European Silks in the Ottoman style

▲ **Italian silk damask**
A mid-16th century silk pieced together from several panels, incorporating Ottoman-style tulips and the Islamic motif of hexagonal cartouches. **£400–600/$640–1,000**

Another source of antique textiles is through the dispersal of collections in the auction rooms. Many collections of early silks were assembled in the second half of the 19th century when they were relatively plentiful. Many museums purchased or were given such collections, which were often dispersed by a network of specialist textile dealers. Some were less scrupulous than others in wielding the scissors. Indeed, collections as far apart as Philadelphia, Lyons and London hold parts of the same silk panel. This underlines the fact that antique textiles are important and expensive commodities.

Today, when a collection appears intact on the market, whether a private individual's estate or an important dealer's final stock dispersal, interest will be strong from institutions and private collectors.

In the 16th and 17th centuries, as the Italian silk industry was starting to be eclipsed by the French, Italian silk merchants saw an opportunity for expansion into the Ottoman market. They proceeded to weave velvets brocaded with ogival cartouches in gold threads of the kind that the Ottoman Empire was producing for the court.

There are some important stylistic differences. Gilt loops in the velvet pile are an Italian feature. In the Ottoman velvets, slight changes are caused by minute variations in the natural dyes, whereas in Italian "Ottoman" silks, the colour changes are woven in: if you look carefully, you will see that the colour changes are regular, rather than spontaneous. Italian weavers also wove silk damasks for the Ottoman market, whereas Ottoman weavers did not. From the 17th century onwards, the French also exported to the Ottoman market, especially *yastik* covers in traditional Ottoman patterns, and woven dress silks.

▶ **Silk panel**
An impressive panel of Italian silk
painted with neo-classical motifs
and dating from the 1780s.
£400–600/$640–1,000

▼ **Gentleman's night cap**
Such caps were intended to be worn in the
evening once the owner had retired to his study
and removed his wig – this is a particularly fine
silk example.
£300–500/$480–800

▶ **Length of silk**
A fine 17th-century piece
brocaded with hunting scenes.
£1,500–2,000/$2,400–3,200

# Italian Silks

With the waning of trading empires such as Venice, Genoa and Florence came the slow decline of the Italian silk industry. However, in the 17th century, Italy still produced first-class silks and velvets and also continued to export them. The golden age of Italian silk production was certainly from the middle of the 14th century until the end of the 17th century. At this point, the French silk industry took over not only the Italian home market but also their export markets. In fact, the debt owed by the French to the Italians is clearly to be seen in the names of the French silks for instance *gros de Naples*.

The sumptuary laws instigated by Colbert in France in 1660 had far-reaching effects on the Italian silk industry, preventing orders being placed in Italy for the French court. Although Italy continued to produce flowered silks, most were for the domestic market, and the Italians concentrated on the production of furnishing textiles. In this field they excelled; Italian velvets between 1670 and 1750 were

the finest in Europe, and Genoese velvets were particularly prized. High-quality damasks were equally famous, and Italian furnishing damasks, as opposed to dress damasks which were produced in some quantity in all silk centres, remained popular until the end of the 18th century without any significant rival.

Colours were obtained using deep, vegetable dyes. Crimson predominated, with green and blue as ground colours. Yellow was generally used as a highlight, often in combination with red, where it simulated the effect of metal thread. For a clear idea of how these textiles were used, you should study a painting of the period, such as a nativity scene. The Virgin will be wearing the most costly silks, and the stable will be hung with tapestries and velvets.

The types of textiles produced were dictated by market demand. There were three main functions for Italian silks from the 17th to 19th centuries: for the Church, the home, and for costumes. The first function was led by religious requirements. The

▼ **Length of red silk damask**
Woven with urns of flowers in c.1700.
Formal patterns such as these continued
to be revived well into the 19th century.
**£500–1,000/$800–1,600**

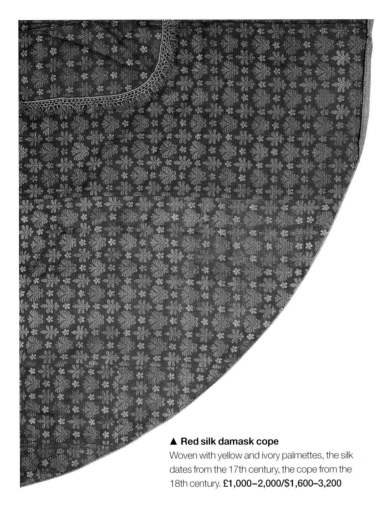

▲ **Red silk damask cope**
Woven with yellow and ivory palmettes, the silk
dates from the 17th century, the cope from the
18th century. **£1,000–2,000/$1,600–3,200**

Catholic church commissioned and used silks extensively in this period, and even within private houses textiles with religious motifs were frequently used as a form of interior decoration.

The second function was led by the demands of the Italian aristocracy for furnishings. The aristocracy began to use hangings which were specifically designed for use in a domestic setting, and were therefore usually embroidered rather than woven. The silks were mounted on *batons* as we would today use wallpaper. Damasks were particularly successful in this respect and formed the backbone of the Italian silk industry into the 18th and even 19th centuries.

In the 17th century, the use of silks in costume changed from large draped panels to closer-fitting clothes. Italian silk patterns of the 18th century were rather more conservative than their French equivalents and so changed rather less as the century progressed. In the early 19th century, Italian design is less easy to define as it followed more closely the example of fashionable contemporary French silks. However, the mid-19th century saw a revival in Italian style, with a move towards a flamboyant taste which included a preference for gilt and classical splendour, a characteristic which remains to this day.

The collector can therefore expect to find long lengths of damask, particularly red, as large quantities were produced at the time. It can be found in more or less good condition depending on its history. Less common colours, such as blue and green, command a premium. In the first decade of both the 18th and the 19th century, canary yellow also became fashionable.

Collectors are fairly constant in their search for good Italian textiles. The home market is particularly strong and is well informed about the international marketplace. In addition to collectors, Italian textile designers are very active in searching out historic textiles as inspiration for contemporary fabrics. Both these factors can make a good Italian silk more expensive than, for example, its Spanish equivalent.

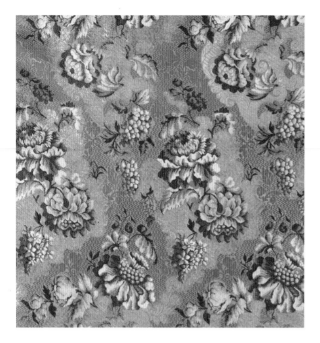

**▲ Detail of a length of silk**
This flowered silk is in the manner of Jean Revel, the outstanding Lyonnais silk designer of the mid-18th century, and is about 2 metres (6ft 6¾in) square. **£5,000–6,000/$8,000–9,600**

**▼ Young man's silk doublet**
An extremely rare and expensive survival from the early 17th century. **£50,000–100,000/$80,000–160,000**

# Early French Silks

Silk workshops had existed in various French cities such as Reims, Poitiers, Paris and Avignon since the medieval period. During the 15th century, the monarchy tried to develop the industry to counter the prestigious Italian silk imports purchased for the court. In 1536, two Piedmontese merchants set up workshops in Lyons, and Henri IV encouraged further development later in the 16th century. Lyons became a business and financial centre, as well as the setting for fairs where Italian silks were traded.

The development of Lyons as a centre of the silk-weaving industry was helped by the perfection of the drawloom weaving technique there in 1605 by Claude Dangon. This meant that large stylized and symmetrical patterns could be woven in various colourways, rather than just plain silks as had previously been produced. Thus, in the 17th century, the French industry could finally compete with the dominance of the Italian silk trade. Italian taste, however, still prevailed during the 17th century, with symmetrical compositions of bouquets of flowers, foliage or fruit within geometrically shaped ornamental frames of foliage, heraldic motifs or flowers.

The silk industry was promoted in the mid-17th century under Louis XIV's minister Jean-Baptiste

Colbert. In 1667, he published an ordinance creating *La Grande Fabrique*, a corporation for craftsmen within the silk industry, and Lyons became the undisputed French silk capital. Controls were exerted to regulate quality and price, embargoes were placed on the importation of foreign silks and sumptuary laws enacted to regulate the consumption of silk products. From 1666, the royal household regularly placed orders to furnish and maintain royal residences and therefore support the industry. The obsession with fashion and interior design provoked a prolific expansion in silk-weaving over the course of the 18th century. In Lyons, there were 3,000 weavers in 1660, but this had increased to 20,000 by the time of the French Revolution in 1789. Under Louis XIV, France was becoming the dominant force in Europe in matters of fashion and style. This led to a gradual distancing from the pervasive Italian taste and to the development of a specifically French style, which came to fruition in the early 18th century.

It is very rare for silks to survive from this period. We know that commissions were received from the royal household for sumptuous silks brocaded with gold and silver, but only through archive documents, as none of the actual pieces appear to remain in

**▲ Ivory satin**
A length of attractive ivory satin, woven with stylized
coral swags, dating from the 18th century.
**£500–550/$800–900** per metre (39½in)

# Collecting
# *Philippe de Lasalle*

**▲ Seat cover designed by Philippe de Lasalle**
Depicting peacocks and game birds, dating from c.1773.
**£1,000–1,500/$1,600–2,400**

existence. Some polychrome and brocaded pieces
survive in dress examples from the 17th century, but
again, these are extremely unusual. Monochrome silk
damask lengths, in red, yellow or green, or a combination of two of these colours, tend to survive in the
largest numbers. Used mainly for upholstery and
wall-coverings, the patterns echo the general silk
designs of the period. Such silk damasks remained
popular during the 18th and 19th centuries, and this
may account for their survival rate. Examples from the
second half of the 17th century can be distinguished
from later pieces, both by the quality of the weaving
and the scale of the design. The designs tend to be
larger and bolder than 18th-century pieces, using the
formal and stylized vocabulary of 17th-century silk
design.

As with all silks, those in original condition – that
is in complete lengths, from selvedge to selvedge in
width, and with several repeats of their pattern in
length – are most sought after by collectors. Most
surviving pieces today have joins or piecing, where
panels of the same silk have been added on but the
repeat is not quite complete. Those in optimum
condition, without too many joins, splitting and
staining, are extremely desirable to textile collectors.

Philippe de Lasalle (1723–1804) was one of the
most distinctive designers of French silks
during the 18th century. He was an artist, weaver,
silk merchant and technician, developing and
improving many silk-weaving techniques. He
trained under the artist François Boucher and
received his silk-weaving mastership in 1749.

He came to prominence in the 1760s, developing a very personal style that was soon much
copied. This moved away from the contemporary Rococo style to a greater centrality and
weight, with simple, understated forms which
anticipated the neo-classical style. He often used
animals and birds, such as lambs, pheasants,
partridges and doves, as well as naturalistic
flowers, in detached compositions.

He also used portraits and figures, often
enclosed within suspended medallions, with an
almost embossed effect. He was a master of the
brocading technique, using black and purple
outlines to create a relief effect, and depth and
shading to give a three-dimensional appearance.

He had many clients in France and abroad,
including the Polish court, and was also commissioned by Empress Catherine II of Russia.
Although he was ruined by the French
Revolution, his work heralded the designs of
the late 18th and early 19th centuries. Today,
his work is still highly sought after as a representation of the pinnacle of silk-weaving and design
in France during the 18th century.

▲ **Length of brown silk**
Brocaded with large-scale
flowers and pagodas,
1730s. The leafy roses are
typically French in style.
**£500–£1,000/$800–1,600**

▲ **Length of silk brocade**
Woven in the 1720s with typical "floating island" motifs of a
monument in a garden, surrounded by outsize pomegranates
and swagged drapery. **£500–1,000/$800–1,600**

◀ **Length of silk damask**
A red and ivory silk from the 18th
century, woven with acanthus
leaves and palmette flowers.
**£500–1,000/$800–1,600**

# 18th-Century French Silks

The French silk industry was closely linked to the fortunes of the rulers of France, and political and economic events affected it dramatically. For example, royal orders were suspended in the early 18th century as a result of wars and famine, until the death of Louis XIV in 1715. However, production was maintained and designs continued to evolve, catering to the taste for novelty at the time.

In the late 17th and early 18th century, Italian style was still predominant, reflected in "bizarre" silks. These were woven with long repeat lengths, sometimes up to a metre (39⅜in) long. The designs comprised strange asymmetrical patterns, hence the name, often incorporating oriental motifs and exotic flowers, and usually in brilliant colour combinations such as pink, green and brown.

In the 1730s, the first truly French style emerged with the designer Jean Revel (1684–1751). He produced designs with outsize naturalistic fruit and flowers that dwarfed other surrounding motifs such as

architectural ruins, shells, figures and oriental-inspired patterns. He is said to have invented the technique of *points rentrés*, where tones of colour of the silk brocade were dovetailed so that the division was less severe and a three-dimensional effect could be achieved with shading. The influence of the Rococo was felt in the 1740s and 1750s, with trailing meanders across plain or diapered grounds. Flowers were stylized, unlike contemporary English silks where more naturalistic patterns were being developed.

With the archaeological discoveries throughout Europe during the mid-18th century, neo-classical influences soon became apparent in French textiles. Meanders turned into stripes, and patterns generally became more geometric and simplified. *Chiné*, or warp-printed silk, was also popular from the 1760s, the process giving a watered or blurred effect to the design. The popularity of painted and embroidered silks also affected the silk industry. These silks cost as much as woven silks and were highly sought after.

◀ **Suit of powder-blue silk**
This suit comprising three pieces is woven *à disposition* (to shape) with borders simulating entwined lace and floral ribbons, 1760s.
£10,000–12,000/$16,000–19,200

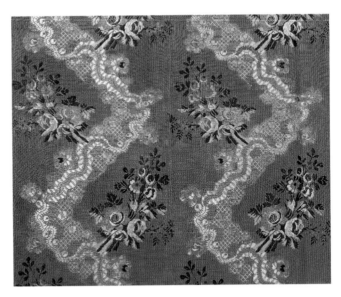

▲ **Rose pink silk panel**
This kind of silk enjoyed a revival in the 19th and 20th centuries, so the width must be checked to attribute a date in the 18th century.
£500–1,000/$800–1,600 for an 18th-century piece
£100–150/$160–240 for a 19th-century piece

In the second half of the 18th century, there began to be more of a division between dress and furnishing silks. Dress silks became simpler, reflecting current fashions, while furnishing silks retained larger patterns and bold neo-classical motifs. Designs necessarily remained more striking than those used for dress silks, and stayed in fashion for a longer period. This did not stop silk manufacturers producing new collections twice a year in the early 18th century, however, rising to four times a year later in the century to cater to ever-changing tastes.

There were other centres of the silk industry in France apart from Lyons, but they tended to specialize in types of silk. For example, Tours produced a ribbed silk known as *gros de Tours*, while Nîmes, Avignon and Paris produced plain silks that appealed to more middle-class tastes. It was the luxury end of the market in Lyons, however, that attracted the best designers, whose names sum up 18th-century French silk design. Apart from Revel and Philippe de Lasalle (*see* p.67),

Jean Pillement, Camille Pierre Pernon, and Jean David Degourc all produced silks that are especially prized today.

The Revolution dealt a severe blow to the social and economic structures that had promoted and maintained the silk industry. However, the industry picked up again in 1795 due to a commission from the Spanish court, and the Directoire style of 1794–9 redefined and simplified the neo-classical style for further development in the 19th century.

French design had such an influence on other silk-producing centres in Europe that it can be quite difficult to pinpoint origin, although there are general differences between English and French silks. French brocaded colouring tends to be more pastel than the brighter, fresher colours used in England. Also, French silks tend to be slightly wider than their English counterparts, although it is difficult to generalize. Original lengths of silk, without joins or damage, are rare and fetch very high prices on the open market.

▼ **Silk chasuble**
This silk brocade woven with roses suggests the 18th century, but the width of the fabric and the drawing of the roses make a 19th-century date more likely. **£200–300/$320–480**

▲ **Length of ivory satin**
Brocaded with sinuous poppies recalling fabrics made for couturier Charles Worth in the 1890s. **£400–600/$640–1,000**

▲ **Length of silk damask**
Again, this damask is in an 18th-century style, but was woven in the 19th century. **£500–1,000/$800–1,600**

# 19th-Century French Silks

After the hiatus in silk production in France caused by the French Revolution, the industry was re-invigorated by Napoleon and by the technological developments of the Industrial Revolution.

Napoleon Bonaparte took up the role of promoting French industry, much as the monarchy had done prior to the Revolution. Lyons received various commissions from him, as he set about re-furbishing royal residences. The number of these had actually increased with the expansion of the Empire, including residences in Florence, Brussels, Rome and Strasbourg. Versailles was also restored in 1807. This secured the future of the silk industry and its output of luxurious furnishing textiles.

The designs of the early 19th century are strongly neo-classical, alluding to the current political situation and its parallels with the classical past, as well as a continuation of developments of the late 18th century. Popular motifs include wreaths of laurel and myrtle, oak leaves, stars, trophies, shields, acanthus leaves and bees, Napoleon's personal symbol. The imperial eagle and the initial "N" were used more rarely. These motifs were often depicted against vivid coloured

grounds including tones of yellow, lilac, blue, green, red and orange. Floral designs were also used, again a continuation of 18th-century trends, usually either scattered, or as wreaths or bouquets. Popular flowers included roses, poppies and lilies of the valley.

With the restoration of the monarchy, further renewal of the royal residences was undertaken by Louis XVIII in 1815 to strip away imperial symbols and reassert the new political order. Private orders also increased from aristocrats, wealthy bourgeois and the newly rich who, now able to afford such luxuries, were building and restoring mansions. Silk textiles had become accessible to a wider clientele with technological progress and subsequent reductions in price. The major innovation of weaving was the Jacquard head attachment, which provided a mechanical means of raising warp threads by a series of punched cards.

Artificial dyes were also developed in the early 19th century. These were more dependable and less expensive than natural ones. A more resilient silk thread also helped the weaving process, and royal commissions under Louis XVIII and Charles X helped investigate and promote these advances in an

◀ **Length of brocade**
Although the motifs are typical of the 18th-century designer Philippe de Lasalle, the colour scheme is 19th-century.
**£1,000-1,500/$1,600–2,400**

▶ **Louis XVI-style silk brocade**
This pink and ivory striped pattern was popular in the late 19th century.
**£100–200/$160–320**

◀ **Length of yellow silk**
The canary-yellow dye for this silk was introduced in the opening decade of the 19th century.
**£500–600/$800–1,000**

industry that was seen as a very important part of France's manufacturing output.

In the 1830s, a new style of design emerged in reaction to the pervasive neo-classicism. It was a nostalgic romanticism that plucked ideas from various centuries from the Middle Ages to the 18th century. Louis Philippe, who reigned from 1830 to 1848, decided to refurbish all his royal palaces in their original style. This led to a blend of styles and a reliance on supposed historical designs rather than new design developments. Gothic elements, such as pointed arches, and mythical creatures, such as dragons, are typical of this period.

The Second Empire (1852–70) was a period of remarkable prosperity. The industry diversified further as silks began to be made for a specific use, such as vestments, upholstery and dress fabrics. New silk textiles were developed including crêpes, gauze and taffeta. International exhibitions in Paris promoted the industry and also inspired designers, and became increasingly important and prestigious showcases in the second half of the 19th century, as the French industry faced mounting foreign competition.

The 1870s marked a watershed, with war and the collapse of the Second Empire and subsequent economic crisis. New inspiration was needed, and perhaps this was not really found until the 1920s and ascendance of firms such as Bianchini-Férier.

The Art Nouveau style did not have much impact on French silk design at the end of the century. Silk manufacturers began to collaborate with *haute-couture* designers such as the House of Worth. Silks were produced with large-scale naturalistic floral designs and other patterns based on natural phenomena such as clouds, swallows and stalactites, showing the pervasive influence of Japanese design. Some designs had overtly oriental references, such as chrysanthemums. These were often made up by Worth into elaborate evening gowns. Lengths of silk from this period can be recognized from the large scale of the motifs used and the generally spacious way in which they are placed, leaving large amounts of the ground, often satin, visible. This collaboration with the burgeoning Paris *haute-couture* industry continued into the 20th century and safeguarded the future production of silk textiles in France.

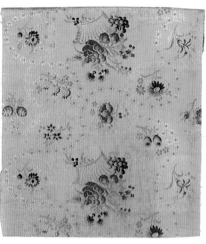

**▲ Length of silk**
A typical 19th-century yellow silk, brocaded with meandering floral ribbons, probably from Norwich.
£100–120/$160–200

**◀ Court robe**
An open robe or mantua worn at court, with silver stripes and naturalistic flowers. Probably made in Spitalfields in the 1750s.
£4,000–5,000/$6,400–8,000

**▼ "Lace-patterned" silk**
A length of impressive dark brown "lace-patterned" silk made in Norwich in the 1720s.
£600–800/$1,000–1,300

# English Silks

The English silk industry developed out of the production of ribbons and half silks in the 16th century. By the middle of the 17th century it was a force to be reckoned with, its growth aided by the demands of the new colony of America and thriving on the stability of the post-Civil War period.

It is said that the silk industry was built up by Huguenots from France, fleeing religious persecution. However, it is probably more accurate to say that they brought business acumen and technical know-how to the native industry. Over time the industry moved from the confines of the City of London where it had been until the mid-17th century, to Spitalfields, on the outskirts. Other important centres were Manchester, nearby Macclesfield, and Norwich.

In England, the silk industry was not as flexible or innovative as in France, and it struggled to keep up with changing fashions. However, the local market was very strong. There was a definite demand for "English" patterns. At the same time, the market was assisted by a series of sumptuary laws, which effectively banned the import of French fabrics. For example, French calicos were banned in 1721, and silks in 1766. In 1773, the Spitalfields Act was passed, agreeing rates of pay with weavers. The resulting industrial peace allowed the English silk industry to flourish until Free Trade reforms came into place at the beginning of the 19th century. The Spitalfields Act was repealed in 1826, leading to an influx of cheap French silks immediately flooding England. The native weavers were unable to compete and the English silk industry collapsed.

An 18th-century English silk was different to its French counterpart in a number of ways. The early 18th century saw English silk patterns still influenced by the "bizarre" silks of the late 17th century, and the earliest designs of the Huguenot James Leman, of around 1707, show this influence and those of Japanese and Chinese designs. At this point, the French and English designs begin to become more distinct.

In the 1720s one can see a strong sense of movement in the patterns, with the characteristic naturalistic flowers appearing among undulating ribbons. The feel in the hand is of a very flexible silk,

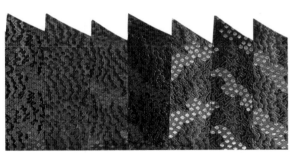

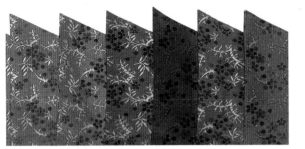

and a botanist can tell you the Latin names of many of
the flowers on English silks, so accurately are they
drawn. A contemporary French silk flower would
tend to be more of a fantasy bloom.

The mid-1740s were the period of English Rococo,
with accurate botanical detail against plain grounds,
usually on a smaller scale. By the end of the decade,
patterned grounds were fashionable. The next
decades saw continued trailing designs, with ribbons
of lace, undulating among more stylized flowers.
Lace-patterned silks continued to be fashionable for
some time. Silk was also partly woven with metal
thread, to provide the stiff texture required for the
voluminous skirts of formal robes.

In the 1770s fashions changed dramatically to a
more fluid line, and silks became lighter and more
drapable. Stripes appeared with neo-classical wreaths,
rosettes, ovals and more pastel shades. Paper taffeta
and satins became popular. The silks of the 1780s can
be almost abstract, and are sombre in tone. By the end
of the 1790s, gauzes and lightweight figured silks were
enveloping the fashionable young lady.

# Collecting Anna Maria Garthwaite

Anna Maria Garthwaite (1689/90–1763)
was the most important designer of silks
in Spitalfields. She was the daughter of Ephraim
Garthwaite, a parson from Grantham in
Lincolnshire, and his wife Rejoyce.

After her father's death in 1719, Anna Maria
lived in the household of her aunt, who had
married Robert Danny, the Rector of Spofforth,
near York. Anna Maria doubtless followed the
pursuits required of a well-brought-up parson's
daughter, particularly needlework and water-
colour painting.

By 1729 or 1730 she was sending silk designs
to London. She moved there with her widowed
sister in 1730 and lived in Spitalfields until her
death in 1763. She worked as a designer for
various mercers and weavers, and was able to
design for particular weaves. Many of her designs
are labelled with the number of shuttles required
and the colour changes required, and show a
high degree of technical knowledge.
Throughout her career, her love of flowers
remained evident in her designs, despite her
knowledge of other styles and influences.

Many of her pattern books were acquired in
the 1860s by the Victoria & Albert Museum in
London, and form an important design archive.

◀ **Silk lampas panel**
Rare 17th-century Indian silks
of this type were formerly
classified as Assamese – such
pieces are eagerly collected
today, even if damaged as here.
**£3,000–5,000/$4,800–8,000**

▼ **"Trade Embroidery"**
Floor spreads were produced in Gujarat for
export to Europe. The quality of chain stitch
on this example from the 1730s is very high.
**£11,000–15,000/$17,600–24,000**

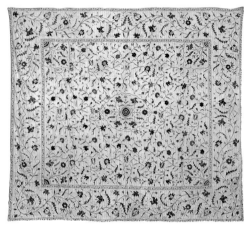

▶ **Velvet cover**
About 2 metres
(6½ft) square, this
piece was intended
to cover a large
dais or platform;
1860s, probably
from Lucknow.
**£800–1,500/
$1,300–2,400**

# Indian Silks

Indian textiles can be roughly grouped into three types for the purposes of collecting: courtly Mughal textiles, "folk" traditional textiles and export textiles.

The court of the Mughal empire (1526–1858) was not fixed but moved from centre to centre. It was not, therefore, bricks and mortar but textiles and tents that surrounded the emperor. As needs dictated, the whole court, complete with its workshops, looms and foundries, would be packed up and moved to a new location. Outer walls of the tents were sturdy and functional, but the wall-hangings and floor spreads, cushions and bedding inside could be very opulent indeed depending on the occupant.

A good number of these inner furnishings have survived from the 17th and, more commonly, from the 18th centuries. These can be in lightweight printed cottons (chintzes) or embroideries, usually taking the form of prayer niches, that is to say a pointed arch with various motifs beneath, often including trees on rocky mounds or single flower sprays. Generally, the simpler the image, the earlier the piece. In the 17th century, the most expensive silks

were those with silver or gold grounds. They are stylistically and technically very similar to Persian brocades of the time and are difficult to tell apart. As in Persia, floral sprig designs predominated with irises, marigolds, roses and poppies the most favoured motifs. These exquisite fabrics were primarily made for court wear, and generally survive in fragmentary form. Such small panels can be relatively inexpensive.

By the 18th century, the city of Benares on the Ganges had developed into an important silk-weaving centre. The most common survivors of this epoch are brocades with deep blue, red or green grounds, woven with gilt spot motifs of small flower buds or *boteh*.

As soon as the various East India Companies had a foothold in the Indian subcontinent, they began to export embroideries and chintzes back to Europe. Indian printed cottons proved to be very popular, and were thought to have magical properties as they seemed to be repainted in fresh colours whenever they were washed. European dyes were not so colourfast.

The province of Gujarat in north-western India was an important centre, producing embroideries of

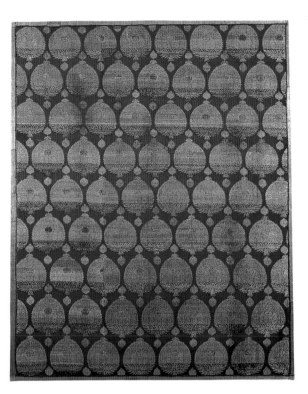

**▲ Silk brocade**
A silk and metal thread brocade from Benares, about 111 by 134 cm (43½ by 52¾in) – each *boteh* is in the form of a small shrub, *c.*1800. **£1,000–1,500/$1,600–2,400**

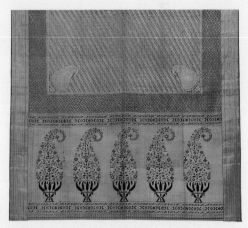

**▲ Sari, probably from Benares in the 1850s**
Shown here is the typical elaborate *pallu*, or end border, seen to advantage draped over the shoulder.
**£100–120/$160–200**

all formats for the European market. The most famous are its chain-stitch embroideries. Usually produced on fine Indian cotton (so fine that it almost feels like silk), these embroideries are so delicate that they can on first inspection be taken for chintzes. Gujarat had Portuguese connections and so also produced embroideries in the Portuguese style, complete with coats of arms in some cases.

Generally, Indian embroideries are executed on a cotton or silk ground. However, the English also exported linen and cotton mixes (fustians) to India to be embroidered and then brought home. Usually, these were in the form of bedcovers or floorspreads, often with a central ogival medallion with corner medallions. However, by the late 18th century, you might also find dress fabrics, including white-on-white and chain-stitched muslins for the fashionable European muslin dresses.

Indian textiles were superseded in Europe in the 19th century by the indigenous printed cottons, and soon the direction of the trade temporarily flowed from Manchester to India rather than vice versa.

At present very few collectors have turned their attention to saris, so they can still be acquired very reasonably. Some of the most technically complex come from Gujarat, in north-western India, and are woven in double ikat technique. This means that not only are the warp threads pre-dyed with a pattern, but also the wefts. Lining up patterns correctly is a technical marvel. These saris are known as *patolas*. A large number were woven for export to Indonesia. Their colour range is always red, green, yellow, brown and ivory. Export *patolas* often include elephants and tigers in their characteristic lattice field.

One type of sari that is already sought after is the wedding sari from the town of Surat, north of Bombay, stitched for the Parsee community by Chinese embroiderers, and known as Gara saris. They are usually worked on dark blue or maroon silk gauze. In perfect and unworn condition, they are presented to the bride at the wedding ceremony. They then become a treasured part of her trousseau, and rarely reappear on the market: the supply is therefore limited despite the high demand from collectors.

For value for money, the canny collector should take a look at the gold and silk saris of Benares. Woven in warm colours and brocaded with gold thread *boteh*, they are a reminder of hot days and brilliant sunshine, and yet are very inexpensive outside India.

# Velvets

## From the 14th century on: complex textiles providing magnificence for Church and State

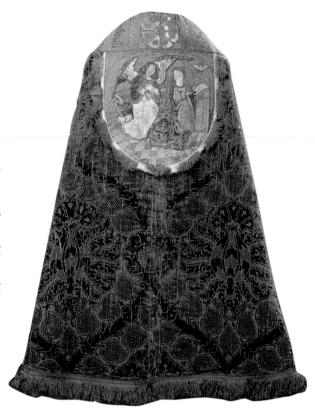

The creation of velvet requires a highly complex and sophisticated weaving technique. The ground weave, the pile and any additional embellishment, such as brocading, are all produced at the same time. The silk industry was first introduced to Italy and Spain by their Islamic invaders in the Middle Ages. The Italian silk-weaving industry was one of the only places in Europe that had developed the technology to carry out the manufacture of velvet textiles by the 13th century.

The political structure of Italy in the 14th century – that of competing city states – meant that cities vied with each other to set up valuable silk industries. Centres were established in Genoa, Venice, Lucca and Florence, although Lucca saw a decline in its fortunes during the 14th century. Velvet was an integral part of the industry, being highly prized across Europe.

During the 14th century, inspired by Eastern imports, patterns began to be worked into the texture. To begin with, these were basic stripes and checks, but by the mid-14th century velvet with simple floral patterns in gold was, for example, produced. In the early 15th century, velvets and silks were woven with plant and animal designs with a strong diagonal axis forming distinct bands. Repeats were still small, in the range of 12–15cm (4–6in) wide.

Complex brocading skills were developing which meant that velvet panels could be enriched with coloured silks, gold threads and gold weft loops. There was also a technical change in the weaving of cloth of gold in the 1430s. Wefts of yellow silk, mainly visible on the rear, were used instead of gold. This meant broad expanses of cloth of gold could be produced less expensively.

The combination of cloth of gold and velvet was the apogee of Italian velvet-weaving. Textures could be emphasized by cut and uncut pile, where warp pile loops are cut or not, and also by pile-on-pile velvets, where pile was of differing heights, creating a three-dimensional relief effect. By the 16th century, the pomegranate motif typical of the Italian Renaissance was still used but was gradually being replaced by voluminous foliage. The ogee lattice of enclosing branches was the principal design

◀ **Velvet cope**
This superb 16th-century cope with an embroidered hood is woven with ogival medallions. Such velvets are usually found only as parts of ecclesiastical vestments.
£5,000–8,000/
$8,000–12,800

▼ **Velvet chasuble**
Woven with green piled leaf lattices on yellow satin, this chasuble shows the smaller repeats that were common by the 17th century.
£1,000–1,500/$1,600–2,400

▶ **Red chasuble**
The pattern of the red Genoese voided velvet is etched into the pile on this 15th-century chasuble – green and blue versions are much rarer. £4,000–6,000/
$6,400–10,000

motif of the 16th century. Designs were increasingly based on ornamental features such as vases, grotesques and birds. They also came to rely less on textural variations and more on colour contrasts such as red and cream or green and yellow, rather than the monochrome, whether red or green, as previously used for velvet.

As the 16th century progressed, designs also became increasingly geometric and on a much smaller scale, with small stylized floral sprigs, slashes and broken branch motifs. This continued into the first half of the 17th century. Velvet was also used as a ground for appliqué work, as seen in surviving ecclesiastical panels and runners.

The establishment of silk industries in France and England during the 17th century, and the political measures used to protect them, hit the Italian silk industry hard. The leading edge of design and production passed from Italy to France and was never regained. Although still producing velvets and silks, Italian designs tend to be more dependent on French ideas and tastes. Italian velvet was still highly prized and Genoese *Jardinière* velvets were highly sought

after between 1670 and 1750 – the name reflects the strong pattern of flowers. They were monochrome in blue or in kermes red, a scarlet red produced from the qirmiz or shield louse, or frequently in both red and green against an ivory satin ground, with varying heights of pile. The flowers were simply drawn on a bold scale and the velvets were often used for the upholstery of fashionable rooms of the time. The kermes gave the red a pinkish tinge which distinguishes it from French and English imitations in the same style.

Today, early Italian velvets are highly desirable to collectors who recognize their workmanship and rarity. They were produced as luxury items for the wealthiest members of European society, and this is reflected both in the materials used and the magnificence of the designs. Occasionally panels of velvet can be found, along with smaller fragments, but the best-preserved pieces tend to be ecclesiastical vestments. Such chasubles and copes display the stunning opulence of Italian Renaissance velvet and are as keenly sought after by collectors today as by their original patrons.

▲ **Moroccan wall hanging**
A 19th-century wall-hanging of silk velvet with appliqué arches. Prices of such pieces, called "Haiti" in Arabic, can rise sharply if decorative interests are aroused. **£1,800–2,500/$3,000–4,000**

◀ **Persian floor cover**
This 19th-century velvet floor cover, with typical motifs, is woven with silk pile on a cotton foundation. **£500–1,000/$800–1,600**

# Indo-Persian Velvets

Both Iran (formerly Persia) and India have long and illustrious traditions of weaving velvets. The two countries thus not only share design vocabulary, but also the skill of creating velvet. It can therefore be difficult to decide if a velvet is Indian or Persian. However, some technical differences have recently been discovered which suggest that Persian velvets reveal their structure on the reverse of the fabric by showing diagonal lines, whereas Mughal velvets have a plain back. These lines are caused by the proportions of picks to warps – the patterns used on these diagonal velvets do also seem to be Persian in design. However, there is no technical reason why either Persian or Indian weavers should not, on occasion, have reversed the proportions of their weaving.

The Persian tradition of velvet predates the Mughal. The Mughal Emperor Jehangir, who reigned from 1605 to 1628, was proud of being able to trace his ancestry back to Shah Tahmasp of Persia, and had himself painted surrounded by celebrated Persian ancestors. The court was surrounded by royal workshops producing goods, and the production of textiles was highly regulated. Only certain ranks were allowed to purchase the most expensive velvets, and textiles acted to some extent as an alternative currency.

Their main purpose was to be made into fabulous robes of honour for the court. Persian miniatures of the 16th and 17th centuries clearly show courtiers wearing recognizable velvets. The large scale of the repeat in 16th- and 17th-century velvet, however, suggests that it may also have been intended to be viewed flat, rather than draped or cut. Velvets were certainly used as wall-coverings when exported to Europe.

The cost of these textiles was enormously high, particularly given that their high metal content would have consisted of real silver and gold, and that enormous skill was required to weave them. In fact, in the 1660s velvet woven with metal thread (called *zerbaft I makhmal*) was said to be the most expensive fabric in the world, according to the traveller Sir John Chardin – this is still the case today. Examples of 16th-century Persian velvets come to auction only rarely and can fetch staggering sums.

There is a very small group of silks and velvets in various techniques which bear the signature of Ghiyath the Weaver. Research shows that he was a trusted courtier of Shah Abbas I, and he is the only weaver known to sign his name. Little else is known about him, or whether he worked in either of the two major centres of Yazd or Isphahan. Nor is it known whether he wove

► **Persian velvet robe, 16th century**
Woven with elegant courtiers among flowers, this
is virtually priceless – an uncut length of similar
velvet recently sold for **£750,000/$1,200,000**

▼ **Silk ikat velvet**
A velvet from Bokhara in the 1880s – technical
difficulties made such velvets unviable despite
their beauty. **£1,000/$1,600** per metre (39½in)

▲ **Ottoman velvet**
A fine example of a classic weaving – related
examples are sought by all important collections.
**£35,000–50,000/$56,000–80,000**

signed pieces himself or simply designed them. These
velvets are extremely rare and expensive.

Persian velvets began to decline in quality and
design in the 18th and early 19th centuries, although
fine pieces were still being made for the élite. By the
end of the 19th century, the quality of silk decreased,
and mixtures with cotton appeared. By the 1880s,
Persian velvets had also made the transition from
sublime pictorial velvets of silver, gold and silk to utilitarian prayer arches in silk and cotton velvet, in aniline
purple and emerald green dyes.

In 17th-century India, the Mughal emperors had
instituted a highly organized luxury textile production
within the palace workshops on the Persian model. In
the case of the Mughal empire, this was particularly
impressive, as the court itself was peripatetic, moving
around the realm regularly. Textiles were very
important portable scenery, as all the court effectively
lived under canvas. Velvet floor spreads and wall-
hangings were a very practical way of transforming a
tent into a palace. The Emperor's tent was the most
luxurious, with silks, satins, cloth of gold, embroideries and velvets throughout. The rest of the court
also used textiles in the same way, although with pieces
of lesser quality. A relatively large number of velvets

were therefore produced of varying qualities in mobile
weaving studios. Weavers worked alongside metal-
workers, potters and painters, on goods destined
exclusively for the court.

Mughal velvets of the 17th century are particularly
rare. The most interesting pieces appear to have been
woven as small floor coverings. These usually have a
darker border and lighter-coloured field, the border
with arabesques and floral medallions. The design of
the centres is related to contemporary carpet design
and can feature the popular *millefleurs* pattern of Agra
carpets. Complete carpets are extremely rare.

Indian velvets of the 18th century are less interesting in quality and design, as patronage became
more diluted. Some very strange velvets seem to have
emerged in the 18th century in apparently Indian
technique, but woven with Ottoman designs.
Presumably these pieces were designed for export.
However, more research is needed in this area. Velvets
were aimed at a much less select clientele during the
19th century. By the 1860s, the majority are woven
with very few colours and no metal threads, in ikat
technique, usually with a cypress tree in the central
compartment and striped borders. They are still
relatively inexpensive but very decorative.

▲ **Chinese table frontal**
Woven in the 19th century with a dark-blue phoenix against a silver ground, it was attached to a table by the blue cotton band. **£200–500/$320–800**

◄ **Chinese floor spread**
Woven in three strips with classical peonies, bats (synonymous with long life) and lotus flowers, this late 18th- or early 19th-century piece, with leaves woven in metal thread, is *c.* 1.5 by 3m (5 by 10ft). **£1,500–3,000/$2,400–4,800**

# Chinese and Japanese Velvets

Velvet is not simple to weave. However, once the loom is set up with the pre-allocated pile warps in place, all that needs to be done is to weave a simple anchoring weft tightly enough to hold the pile in place once it has been cut (*see* pp.10–11). Chinese weavers were skilful, and able to vary the weft-based techniques to good advantage, using metal thread very effectively as the ground fabric between pile areas. The Chinese were producing superb velvet as far back as the 15th century during the Ming dynasty (1368–1644). Most of the available examples survive in the form of covers for sacred books. Typical of 17th-century Ming velvets are the chequerboard patterns, usually in sombre but rich browns, olive green and burnt orange tones. Embroidered velvet fragments have also reached us, worked with gilt dragon roundels in gold thread.

Velvet seems to have become most popular from the late 17th century on, during the late Ming and early Qing dynasties. Velvets from the Qing dynasty (1644–1911) are many and various. Floor spreads are the most commonly found velvet. Again, deep, sombre colours predominate in the 18th century,

including crimson, dark green and russet. Woven to shape, these pieces typically have a darker border, with the field in lighter-coloured velvet woven with peonies and sometimes dragons and phoenix against a gilt thread ground. These floor spreads appear to have been part of suites of velvet furnishings, which included chair covers in the shape of long, narrow rectangular woven panels. Chair covers are recognized by the fact that the last third of the design is usually upside down in relation to the rest of the piece. This portion is designed to hang over the back of the chair. Chair covers would originally have been woven in numbers of up to twelve. Partly because their use was not obvious to European eyes, these sets have mostly been broken up. They continue to be produced well into the 19th century.

Imperial workshops produced similar products, in imperial yellow velvet, with gold grounds. There is, of course, a premium on any Imperial textile. In the late Qing dynasty, in the late 19th and early 20th centuries, velvet enjoyed a resurgence of popularity in China as a material for making women's robes. A lady would be

◄ **Japanese screen panel**
One of a set of four 19th-century panels woven with beasts of prey.
**£1,200–1,500/$1,900–2,400** for set

▲ **Japanese wrapping cloth**
This 19th-century velvet *fukusa*, or wrapping cloth, depicts the popular subject of chicken and chicks against an uncut ground.
**£500–600/$800–1,000**

◄ **Japanese scroll picture**
A classical scene from nature – the debt to contemporary scroll painting is evident in this 19th-century piece. **£400–1,000/$640–1,600**

required to wear a plain-coloured surcoat over her inner court or informal robe. This was usually of plain, dark blue satin or taffeta. However, velvet woven with dragon or peony roundels became a popular alternative at the end of the century for informal robes.

Without any doubt, Japan reached a high point of technical achievement in the second half of the 19th century. At the same time as they were producing bronzes, porcelain and enamel of stunning technical brilliance, the country's weavers were producing textiles of which no other country was capable.

Unlike most producers, Japan concentrated on large-scale luxury pictorial velvets which had no subsidiary furnishing or clothing use. Large panels were woven for use in folding screens with the narratives continuing over several panels. Hangings over 2 metres (6ft 6¾in) square were produced with the most extraordinary subject matter, such as polar bears sunning themselves on ice flows. More common subjects included tigers and lions in wooded landscapes. The highest-quality velvets relied on woven detail, whereas those destined for slightly less

discriminating clients would have painted details and shading. Landscapes with racing streams, bamboos and pagodas included are probably the most common subject matter.

An interesting group of these velvets is woven with very detailed portraits of dogs, typically the Japanese spaniel. They are usually of small scale, approximately 92cm (36in) square, and often mounted on Japanese silk in deep mahogany frames. They are not only collected by the Japanese but also by dog lovers in general. A good example can outstrip a landscape of three times the size when sold.

As the century progressed, the naturalistic portrayals in Japanese velvets became almost photographic in their detail. Around 1900, Japan began to weave topographical panels, often of Mount Fuji but also of locations outside Japan, and these continued to be produced until the middle of the 20th century. The photographic illusion was underlined by the fact that they were generally woven in black and white only. These pictures have not yet been widely collected and are still very affordable.

▲ **Velvet floor spread**
Made in 1811–12 for the apartments of the Empress Marie
Louise at Versailles. **£400–800/$640–1,300**

◄ **Velvet panel**
A furnishing velvet, woven with neo-classical wreaths and
flowers and embroidered in Lyons by Grand Frères, 1811.
**£500–1,000/$800–1,600**

# French Velvets

The production of velvet textiles in France is closely tied to the French silk industry as a whole. In the late 17th century, Louis XIV had established and promoted the silk industry, eventually gaining predominance over the older-established Italian manufacturers. As the French silk industry came to dominate western Europe, French velvets too came into their own.

Generally patterns follow fairly closely the development in silk brocades during the 18th century (*see* pp.68–9). The *chiné* technique of warp printing was also used to great effect from the 1760s into the 19th century in velvet weaving. *Ciselé* velvet added further relief and shading to the texture in both the 18th and 19th centuries, creating patterns through the combination of cut and uncut pile.

In the late 18th century, velvet was used extensively for gentlemen's formal and court suits. The designs were small scale, often geometric or based on stripes along with stylized foliate motifs, and generally sombre in colour. The effect was usually lightened by elaborate silk embroidery, worked to shape, around the borders. Formal French men's dress continued unchanged into the early 19th century. Such suits in their original condition and which comprise all three pieces – coat, waistcoat and breeches – are very desirable to collectors and can fetch high prices.

From 1790 to 1820, inventors worked with the developing technology. For example, Gaspard Grégoire, whose name is associated with this technique, produced small velvet panels imitating painting. Colour was applied to the silk thread before it was woven into the velvet or painted directly onto the velvet warp. There was a limited level of production due to the intricate technique. Sources were taken from fashionable portraits, landscapes, flowers and antiquity. Motifs were also taken from the recently discovered Herculaneum murals in Italy, placed against a black ground.

Velvet production was affected by the developments of the Industrial Revolution. The cheapness and availability of cotton meant that it was soon used to produce velvet in the 19th century, and so gave the textile a new class of customer. The difference

► **Gentleman's court suit**
Made of chequered velvet and
elaborately embroidered with ears
of corn and poppy seed heads.
A surprising number of these suits
from the 1780–90s have survived.
£700–1,000/$1,200–1,600

▲ **Lyons velvet**
A flamboyant velvet of the 1860s, woven with putti blowing
conch shell horns, from the Mathieu et Bouvard factory, Lyons.
£500–1,000/$800–1,600

◄ **Velvet**
18th century, woven
with silver thread
palmettes and borders.
£300–500/$480–800

between cotton velvet, the most common form today, and silk velvet, is immediately obvious once you have felt the softness of the latter. The appeal of the pile and texture of velvet is readily apparent, and during the 19th century new variations were developed to cater for an increased demand lower down the social scale. Velveteen and plush are two examples, and were used for both furnishing fabrics and dress materials. Velveteen is a close-cut, weft-pile fabric, while plush commonly has a longer and less dense pile than velvet. It generally uses a wool pile against a cotton ground. Prints were also applied to the velvet as a cheaper way of producing a design on the texture, rather than manipulating the pile.

However, the most desirable 19th-century velvets to collectors today remain those produced for the luxury end of the market, predominantly in Lyons. Commissions were received to redecorate mansions, stimulated in part by the increased prosperity under the Second Empire, and, as in the 18th century, designs were necessarily bold. Inspiration in the late 19th century was taken from the Baroque and 18th century, with formal designs incorporating ideas such acanthus scrolls, putti, strapwork and stylized arrangements of flowers. The *ciselé* velvet often used added a depth and texture to the overall effect. Velvet was also used for church vestments produced in Lyons in the second half of the 19th century. Effects were added such as moiré, to give a watered pattern to the surface.

Velvet was often favoured for luxurious evening gowns and was used to emphasize particular motifs such as floral cascades or feathers, against a plainer silk or satin ground. This was particular suited to the larger scale of design elements which developed from the 1860s and was used with great effect by the House of Worth for their evening gowns. A favoured technique was velvet *au sabre,* where the pattern was printed on to the pile warp before weaving. After weaving, the printed areas of pile were then cut away. The technique for weaving such velvets, with combinations of various colours and types of weave, was extremely complex. They were highly regarded by contemporaries and remain so today.

◀ **Velvet robe**
An unnamed velvet
with a spectacular
poppy design,
used upside down.
Velvets of this type
were produced by
Becker & Fils of Paris,
but the tailoring
seems to be amateur.
**£200–300/$320–480**

▲ **Velvet coat by Maria
Monaci Gallenga**
A stylish 1920s coat stamped in
silver, with a frieze of swaying
poppies. **£400–500/$640–800**

▲ **Velvet Fortuny coat**
A chocolate-brown velvet coat
with turquoise padded rouleau
piping, from 1900–20.
**£1,000–2,000/$1,600–3,200**

# 20th-Century Velvets

The production of velvet continued into the 20th century. Cotton velvet and new fabrics such as velveteen contributed to the lower end of the market. Velvets for the luxury market were still produced, concentrated mainly in France and Italy, and these remain the most desirable pieces today for collectors.

Perhaps the most renowned producer of luxury velvets of the 20th century is Mariano Fortuny (1871–1949). He was born in Granada, Spain, into a wealthy artistic family and began his career as an artist. He also studied chemistry and techniques for dying cloth that ultimately led to his distinctive and opulent style. He settled in Venice, in the Palazzo Orfei (now the Museo Fortuny) and his name has become synonymous with that city. In 1922 he opened a factory on the Giudecca island. His velvet textiles were created both as furnishing textiles and to be used as dress fabrics, mainly for over-garments such as mantles and cloaks. He drew his inspiration from many sources, including classical, Ottoman, Renaissance and Arab designs.

A characteristic technique of Fortuny's was to use metallic pigments with which to stencil the pattern against a coloured silk velvet ground. He liked his velvets to look antique and would intentionally create crinkled or flaky effects. The use of stencilling, rather than immersing the velvet in dye, to create the pattern gives his pieces a unique finish and feel. Most of his velvet garments are labelled in the lining, making them relatively easy to identify. The Fortuny label carried on after its founder's death, but later pieces do not generally have the cachet of earlier examples.

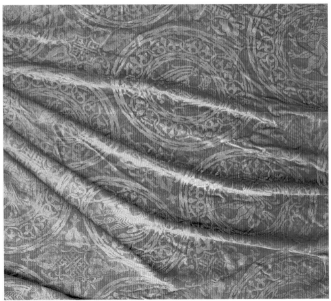

▲ **Velvet bedcover by Maria Monaci Gallenga**
This detail is taken from a large bedcover of rust-coloured silk velvet which is stencilled with Byzantine roundels, and probably dates from around 1920. £1,000–2,000/$1,600–3,200

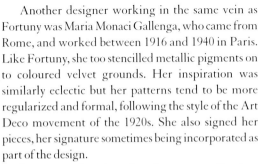

▶ **Velvet evening cape**
A superb "Sorti de Bal" cape of pink velvet by Mario Fortuny stencilled with Gothic palmettes, the hood in contrasting black stencilled velvet. This cape belonged to the New York socialite and model Tina Chow. £5,000–8,000/$8,000–12,800

Another designer working in the same vein as Fortuny was Maria Monaci Gallenga, who came from Rome, and worked between 1916 and 1940 in Paris. Like Fortuny, she too stencilled metallic pigments on to coloured velvet grounds. Her inspiration was similarly eclectic but her patterns tend to be more regularized and formal, following the style of the Art Deco movement of the 1920s. She also signed her pieces, her signature sometimes being incorporated as part of the design.

Lyons continued to be the centre of velvet production for the upper end of the market in France, and various manufacturers, including Bianchini-Férier, benefited from collaboration with leading figures from the world of art and fashion such as Raoul Dufy, Paul Poiret and Cristobal Balenciaga, the latter being Spanish-born and heavily influenced by historical styles. *Devoré* became a popular fabric, especially in the 1920s and 30s. The velvet pile is voided, or removed, to reveal a chiffon ground. The velvet can be worked in several colours to create an elaborate pattern, and the ground is usually in a contrasting colour. It was primarily used for scarves and dresses but sometimes unused lengths can be found, and these are highly valued today.

Luxury pieces, created by a named designer, are highly sought after by both collectors of textiles and collectors of *haute couture* and costume. The early 20th-century velvets have a strong appeal for today's buyers of antique textiles, and if they can be attributed to Fortuny, or to a lesser degree Gallenga, are extremely desirable to collectors.

# Designer Textiles

## From William Morris to Lucienne Day: the rapid growth of designer fabrics

▲ **"Bird" by William Morris**
An example in the less common red colourway, blue and green being more familiar. **£300–500/$480–800** per metre (39½in)

The Arts and Crafts Society grew out of dissatisfaction with the Royal Society of Arts, London in the late 19th century. Sculptors and architects were a small minority within the Royal Society, with little control over the exhibitions that were supported. Seven artists therefore drafted a letter inviting artists and craftsmen to contribute to "an exhibition of the Combined arts", and sixteen met in the Charing Cross Hotel in May 1887, electing Walter Crane as Chairman. The Society ran on very business-like lines, and held its first exhibition in the New Gallery, Regent Street in 1888. Its aims were not exclusively devoted to promoting hand-worked objects, as is commonly thought today – key members of the movement, such as William Morris, introduced machines to produce textiles and carpets.

The artist Ford Madox Brown had first put forward the idea of establishing a decorating firm while working on the interior of the Red House in Bexleyheath, Kent, designed for Morris by Philip Webb. In 1861, Morris, Marshall, Faulkner & Co. was founded, with Morris as the manager. The firm was sustained by stained glass commissions and subsidies until 1865 when Morris came to realize that his means were not sufficient to support the firm – he bought out the other partners, founding Morris & Co. on 25 March 1875. Although the company ran on a deficit for some time, by 1880 chintzes printed by Thomas Wardle were profitable.

In 1881 the firm's headquarters were moved to Merton Abbey, where Morris was able to take full control of the production of woven textiles. By the mid-1880s Morris was more interested in politics, founding the Socialist League, and responsibility for embroideries was passed to his daughter May in 1885, with day-to-day running of the workshops taken over by John Henry Dearle. After Morris's death in 1896 aged 62, Dearle became art director, contributing damask, chintz, carpet and wallpaper designs as well as tapestry and glass patterns until his death in 1932. The firm finally closed in 1940.

Morris & Co. produced a wide range of goods. Embroidery was one of Morris's earliest interests, and there were many named embroideresses, for instance Catherine Holiday, Morris's favourite embroideress, in Arts and Crafts

▼ **"Clover" by Liberty & Co.**
A printed cotton of 1906–9. This kind of print was the staple of the Liberty style at the beginning of the 20th century.
**£200/$320** per metre (39½in)

▲ **"Poppyland" by Liberty & Co.**
A printed cotton of 1912–13. Prints such as this have remained popular with Liberty's customers to this day.
**£150–200/$240-320** per metre (39½in)

exhibitions. Morris and Co. embroideries were shown at the International Exhibition of 1862 to hostile reviews – the popular embroideries of the mid-19th century were predominantly Berlin woolworks. Morris's designs, using the flowers of the English hedgerow worked in wools and silks in a naturalistic manner, seemed shockingly avant-garde. Even so, many embroidery kits were purchased, complete with silks and wools with which purchasers could embroider themselves, or could have patterns made up. Morris's style of embroidery dominated until around 1900, when the sharper, more stylized embroideries of the Glasgow School held sway.

Morris also revived the art of block printing and vegetable dyes. Early patterns, including "Honeysuckle" (1874), "Jasmine Trellis" (1868–70), "Tulip & Willow" (1873) and "Marigold" (1873), featured naturalistic plants, lush leaves and trellises. Morris also produced designs which today look less typical, based on Indian historical textiles. In 1883, Morris was inspired by a 15th-century Italian velvet with a strong diagonal pattern, resulting in designs such as "Evenlode" and "Windrush".

The most influential retailer of the Arts and Crafts movement was undoubtedly Liberty & Co., founded in 1875 by Arthur Lasenby Liberty at 219a Regent Street, London, selling imported Eastern goods. They built on the success of Thomas Wardle's printed silks, buying designs from all the most important designers of the day such as C.F.A. Voysey, Harry Napper, the Silver Studio and Lindsey Butterfield, which were then woven by firms such as Alexander Morton and Warner & Sons. Liberty was particularly important in the spread of Aesthetic Movement costumes. Dresses were loose and worn without constricting corsets. They were considered extremely avant-garde and rather shocking. Jane Morris, William Morris's wife, wore Liberty dresses of which some are now in the Victoria & Albert Museum in London.

In 1890, Liberty opened a branch in Paris and were very successful despite opposition from French manufacturers. Liberty's were responsible for the high regard in which English textiles were held on the continent, and in Italy Art Nouveau is known as Liberty Style.

**▲ Silver Studio design**
This popular design was used for both wallpaper and textiles, and was originally produced for the Silver Studio by C.F.A. Voysey in 1890.
**£500–1,000/$800–1,600** per metre (39½in)

**◀ Silver Studio design**
Another textile design for the Silver Studio, this time from 1899 and by the famous designer Harry Napper.
**£400–600/$640–1,000** per metre (39½in)

**▲ Music stool cover**
Designed by the painter and designer Duncan Grant for Charleston in East Sussex.
**£1,000–2,000/$1,600–3,200**

# Silver Studio, Voysey and Omega

British Textile manufacturers enjoyed a renaissance at the end of the 19th century and beginning of the 20th century. The expanding demand for new designs encouraged the development of design studios such as the Silver Studio. These studios would either sell on the designs to manufacturers or foreign agents, or work up the design themselves. New designs with limited runs gave studios a commercial edge in what was a highly competitive market.

One of the most famous, the Silver Studio, was founded by Arthur Silver in Hammersmith, London, in 1880, closing in 1963, when his son, Rex, retired as head of the business. It was founded to produce repeating designs for furnishing fabrics, wallpapers and floor coverings, but also included other decorative arts such as furniture and metalwork. They recruited various designers: Harry Napper and John Illingworth Kay were among the most notable for textile design, and Archibald Knox for metalwork. Work was unsigned, making it difficult to ascribe it to individual designers today. The leading British textile manufacturers of the time bought designs from them, as well as French and later American manufacturers.

C.F.A. Voysey (1857–1941) had a prolific career as a designer that lasted for over fifty years. His earliest recorded design dates from 1883 for the wallpaper firm, Jeffrey & Co. In 1895, he won a contract with the well-known textile manufacturer Alexander Morton to produce ten exclusive textile designs per year. He also sold designs to other leading manufacturers of the era and shops such as Liberty's.

His decorative style was formed during the 1880s and 1890s and drew from disparate influences including A. W. N. Pugin, William Morris and Walter Crane. He disapproved of the Art Nouveau style that was developing during the 1890s, believing instead in simplicity and in the avoidance of all unnecessary embellishment. He developed a recognizable personal style, grounded in but not dependent on tradition. He used simple two-dimensional shapes and elegant flowing curves, and made repeated use of stylized bird motifs, sometimes in pairs, as well as other animals which generally appear in silhouette. Dragons, angels and sea-creatures also feature in his designs, and he took the heart as his personal symbol. Flowers and trees were treated in a similar manner, stylized and

▲ **"White"**
A printed linen produced by the Omega Workshops in 1913. This design was ahead of its time, and could easily be mistaken for a textile design from the 1950s.
**£400–600/$640–1000** per metre (39½in)

▼ **Silver Studio velvet**
A roller-printed cotton velvet from 1898 using a typical motif by Alphonse Mucha, a leading figure in the Art Nouveau movement, who devoted himself to painting from 1903.
**£1,000–1,500/$1,600–2,400** per metre (39½in)

often in silhouette, giving an economy of line and sense of space that appeared very modern for the time.

Voysey understood the technology behind the production of his designs and often noted special technical instructions on his original drawings. He also updated and transposed his ideas between technologies. He designed for his entire life although his style did not alter radically in the early 20th century, maintaining that established at his peak in the 1890s. However, he did work on more narrative themes, especially for the nursery, and the dispersal, size and colouring of his motifs showed some evolution.

The Omega Workshops was a design company founded by the artist Roger Fry in 1913, with Duncan Grant and Vanessa Bell as co-directors. Like the Silver Studio it covered a broad range of decorative arts including furniture, ceramics and textiles. Various artists were employed besides the founders, including Wyndham Lewis. Its primary aim was to apply the aesthetic of post-Impressionism and of Fauvism to British design, which Roger Fry felt had become debased. Its abstract designs challenged the traditional attitudes to pattern-making that were characterized by naturalistic representation. It was also set up to provide a means of income for avant-garde artists.

Its work was publicized through various exhibitions including a post-Impressionist room for the Ideal Home Exhibition of 1913, and also by word of mouth through fashionable London society and artistic and intellectual circles. Their client list consisted of many avant-garde artists and thinkers of the time including Picasso, André Derain and Gertrude Stein.

The Workshop's style was characterized by abstract design, bold colours, black defining outlines and undyed grounds, reflecting the art that was also being produced by the artist/designers within the group. The keynote was spontaneity and improvisation. Despite some press criticism and accusations of bad production quality, the Omega Workshop attracted successful sales both in England and abroad. Its designs were in advance of their time, and set the fashion for abstract and geometric patterns that were taken up more generally after World War I, aided by the Art Deco movement. The Workshop itself closed in 1919, after declining sales during the war, and as its artists moved on to different projects.

**◀ Design by Marion Mahler**
This abstract pattern was designed for the David Whitehead Ltd in the 1950s by one of its most talented designers.
£50–100/$80–160 per metre (39½in)

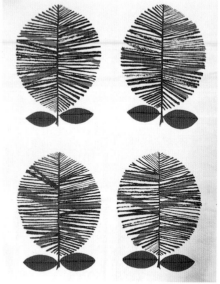

**▲ "Burma" by Sven Fristedt**
A printed cotton from the 1960s produced by Bora Wafvertrieb Scand.
£100–200/$160–320 per metre (39½in)

**◀ "Calyx" by Lucienne Day**
This pattern, designed for the Festival of Britain in 1951 by Lucienne Day, is still desirable today.
£100–200/$160–320 per metre (39½in)

# 1950s and 1960s Textiles

The market for textiles designed in the decades after World War II is continually developing, with specialist sales at auction houses now being set up to cater for the interest in design from this period. Currently, in the textile market, recognizable designs from the 1950s and 1960s are the most highly sought after. Those that epitomize the design movements of these decades are more desirable than the traditional patterns that were continually produced alongside.

The Festival of Britain in 1951 represented a wonderful opportunity for textile designers and manufacturers to showcase their product after the wartime hiatus. Two types of patterns emerged. The first was inspired by science and based on crystal structure diagrams recording arrangements of atoms in substances such as haemoglobin, chalk and insulin. The other developed more abstract forms and organic shapes, inspired by abstract art and artists such as Paul Klee, Joan Miró and Alexander Calder.

This "contemporary" style, as it was christened, went on to have a profound effect for the next decade. Contemporary patterns were predominantly used on furnishing fabrics and printed on to rayon, cotton and linen. The colours used were bright – yellow and red being favourites – against a neutral ground.

Many textile firms in this period commissioned artists to create designs for them that could be adapted for textiles. These included the Edinburgh Weavers Ltd, David Whitehead Ltd and Sanderson Fabrics. In 1960, the British artist John Piper created "Northern

**◀ "Galleria" by Barbara Brown**
A design from *c.*1965 for the department store
Heals in London, a leading force in textiles in the
1960s. **£200–300/$320–480** per metre (39½in)

**▼ "Hourglass" by W. Herzberger**
A design for the British firm of Turnbull and
Stockdale from 1954, with colours typical of
the period. **£50–100/$80–160** per metre (39½in)

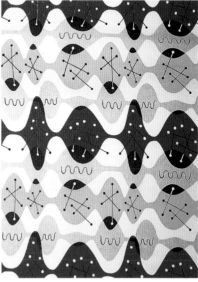

**◀ Op Art design**
The bold geometry of this Op Art design from the
mid-1960s by the Danish designer Verner Panton
aimed to push visual perception to its limits.
**£60–100/$100–160** per metre (39½in)

Cathedral" for Sanderson, which was screen-printed
to give a feeling of the original brush strokes.

From the early 1960s to the early 1970s, large-scale
abstract and geometric patterns were favoured.
Screen printing, which had become mechanized
during the 1950s, enabled costs to be kept low. Op Art
had some influence on textile design, reaching its
height around 1965. While it did not have the
widespread appeal of the contemporary style, the
usually black and white geometric forms, often
creating optical illusions, were popular with the
design establishment. Pop Art was more accessible
with its images based on graphics, kitsch appeal and
humour. These readily translated into textile designs
between the late 1960s and early 1970s, and reflected

contemporary youth culture. The mid-1960s saw the
revival of various historical styles that were updated
with new and more suitable colour palettes, including
psychedelic colours. Inspiration was taken from
sources as diverse as the Arts and Crafts movement,
Art Nouveau, Art Deco and Elizabethan embroidery
designs. This led to repeat patterns of small-scale,
stylized floral and geometric motifs.

Many pieces from this period can still be found at
reasonable prices, although the popularity of 1950s
design in particular has increased dramatically. As
with any period, pieces that can be ascribed to a
particular designer tend to be the most desirable, along
with those that sum up the era, rather than the traditional designs still being produced alongside them.

# Wools

## An introduction: the staple of a nation's economy

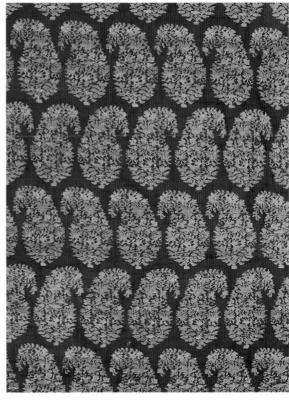

▲ **Panel of woollen cloth**
Woven in dark blue wool with cashmere *boteh*,
probably made in Persia around 1800.
£200–400/$320–640

From the medieval period until the 19th century, Britain had no rival in the production of wool. The industry was widespread across all areas of the country and was the mainstay of economic life for the nation. To begin with, the trade in wool was more important than the manufacture of cloth. Fleeces were sold to countries such as Italy, Germany and the Low Countries, who would then weave the cloth themselves.

As Britain's principal source of wealth, the wool industry enjoyed government privileges including protection by a code of industrial and commercial regulations. In the early 17th century, a proclamation under James I, the effect of which lasted until 1824, prohibited the export of raw wool, ensuring that manufacturers had enough raw material to work with. Wool was produced by weavers working from home in small groups until industrialization began in the late 18th and early 19th centuries. Production then moved to factories and became centralized in certain areas, rather than nationwide, principally in the West Riding of Yorkshire, in towns such as Leeds, Halifax and Huddersfield.

The industrialization of the woollen industry lagged behind that of its main rival, cotton, which by the early 19th century had become increasingly cheap to manufacture. Many innovations used in the mechanization process, such as the spinning jenny, were originally invented for the cotton industry. However, some technical problems in the weaving and combing of fibres for smooth worsted yarn were not overcome until the mid-19th century. With the low cost of cotton, mixed blends were developed by 1830 and by 1858, and it is estimated that 95 per cent of worsted was mixed with cotton. The most rapid period of expansion was between 1850 and 1875, but the real importance of wool to the economy was already in decline with competition from newer industries.

Wool textiles do not survive particularly well, being very susceptible to moths, among

◄ **Tweed suits by Coco Chanel**
Chanel loved English tweed, and even commissioned her own Harris tweed. These suits both date from the 1960s.
**£150–175/$240–280** each

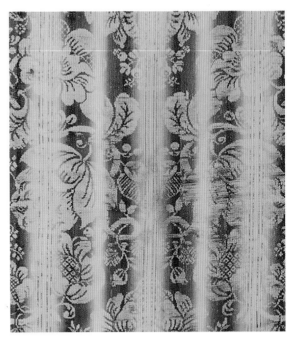

▲ **Norwich wool**
A length of 18th-century striped wool with a floral pattern, woven in Norwich for the Spanish market.
**£500–800/$800–1,300**

other perils. This, along with a perceived inferiority to silk textiles, means that where they do survive they can still be found at reasonable prices. Although there are many different weaves and blends with other textiles, wool can be broken down into roughly three types. In worsted, the yarns are spun from wool combed to lay the fibres parallel, ultimately giving a smooth surface. In woollen cloth, the yarns have fibres that intermingle and lie in all directions, giving a fluffier surface. There is also felt, which is not woven but formed by a process using heat, moisture and compression which causes the fibres to lock together.

There is a bewildering array of terms used to describe the various types and blends of wool popular before 1800. "Linsey-woolsey" was a blend with linen, "camlet" was a worsted cloth which could be stamped with damask patterns in imitation of silk damasks, "calamanco" was a fine worsted cloth, with a glazed surface, usually dyed bright colours and striped or brocaded.

Woollen damasks were also produced, usually copying developments in silk design. They could be plain, usually red, yellow or green, or worked in various colours, as in the length above from Norwich, woven in the mid-18th century. It is thought that this and similar examples were woven for the Spanish export market. Wools could also be used to copy silk brocade, and there are examples dating from the late 18th century, used against a linen ground, which are probably for the French provincial market. These pieces are fascinating for the social and historical background they provide for the development of textile design.

The Arts and Crafts designers also favoured wool textiles – William Morris, for example, revived Utrecht velvet, a woven mohair pile fabric from 17th-century Holland, stamping it with his floral designs. He also used woollen double cloth and blends of wool and cotton. As with any piece connected with Morris, these are highly desired by collectors.

# Tartan

## An introduction: banned for seditious connections, then favoured by royalty

Today, tartan is generally associated with Scotland. However, it is one of the simplest textile designs, and such checked patterns made from two or more colours are found in many cultures. The word "tartan" originally meant a light woollen material of any colour and was derived from the French *tiretaine* or Spanish *tiritana*. It is not a Gaelic word, and there is some discussion as to what word was used to describe such a textile in Gaelic in the past.

There is no evidence that named tartans or clan tartans existed before the mid-18th century. In fact, it would have been impossible to achieve the uniformity associated with clan tartans before this date, as the natural dyes would not give the same shade of colour twice and the hand-weaving processes used were unpredictable. Only with industrialization in the late 18th and early 19th centuries did a general uniformity become obtainable.

This also coincided with immense interest in and romanticization of Scottish life, fostered by the visit of George IV in 1822 and continued by the royal family later in the 19th century,

most famously by Queen Victoria. Highland dress, including tartan, had been proscribed after the Jacobite Rebellion of 1745. The Act was not repealed until 1782, although it does not seem to have been enforced after about 1760. The ending of the proscription brought about a renewed interest in, and curiosity about, Highland dress throughout Britain.

Various publications appeared which formally classified the different clan tartans, the first one being *Scottish Gael* by James Logan in 1831. These books satisfied a demand to know which was the correct tartan to wear. However, there seems to have been no firm clan badge intention in wearing tartan before this date.

William Wilson & Sons of Bannockburn was the major manufacturer of tartan in Scotland, enjoying a monopoly at home and abroad. The company played a large role in promulgating its usage and the systemization of the patterns. It had been founded when Highland dress was proscribed, but they still built up a large export business selling to Scottish colonies and other interested parties. They produced military tartans from 1797 for all the Highland

**▼ Selection of tartans**
Dating from the 18th and 19th centuries, these tartans are a cross-section of military tartans which are not linked to clans but are simply decorative. **£100–200/$160–320** per swatch

**▲ Military dress tartans**
A selection of military dress tartans worn for grand evening functions in the 18th and 19th centuries. **£100–200/$160–320** per swatch

regiments in the British army, and by the early 19th century were producing named clan tartans. In New York in the 1820s, tartans were all the rage, and Wilson's exported over forty clan sets and other named patterns including Glengarry, Glencoe and Prince Royal.

The classification of tartan patterns continued during the 19th and 20th centuries, becoming increasingly complicated. Queen Victoria's extended stays in Scotland helped tartan remain popular, and it was often used for fashionable dress in the mid-19th century, woven in silk as well as wool.

Tartan can be difficult to date accurately, partly because of the nature of the pattern. Clues can be found in the type of dye used, whether it is organic and natural and therefore fairly subdued in colour, or bolder and so later. The width of the wool is also a clue, narrower earlier pieces being woven on individual looms rather than by a mechanized process. It is still possible to find panels of late 18th-century "hard" tartan, made from worsted wool, the smooth surface having a slight sheen. As with all 18th-century wools, it will be tightly woven and

of a completely different quality to the woven wools to which we are accustomed today. The quality is generally so good that raw edges can be left as such without the possibility of fraying.

Tartan pieces associated with royalty are also highly collectable. Those with Jacobite associations can be tricky to date without having a clear provenance. As with collecting any piece associated with a particular person, a definite provenance, particularly with written evidence such as a contemporary letter or note explaining how the items were come by, is preferable to hearsay or an old family story. Queen Victoria's possessions are another example of this, especially as she seems to have been fairly generous in giving gifts to servants and friends.

Dating from the mid-19th century, tartan shawls are also highly sought after by collectors. Their large size, to fit over the wide crinoline, means that today they can still have many uses. Since classification in the early 19th century, the tartan pattern has not changed much, apart from ever-increasing new designs. This means that even tartan from the 19th century will appear relatively contemporary to modern eyes.

# Shawls

## From the 17th to the 19th century: the accessory from India that took Europe by storm

▲ **Spanish stole**
An unusual Spanish stole, embroidered with galleons and probably commissioned in Manilla, 1830s.
£1,000–2,000/$1,600–3,200

The shawl has been a staple of men and women's clothing since cloth was first woven. In India, and particularly in Kashmir, in the shadow of the Himalayan mountains, the shawl became a work of art and a symbol of status. They are known to have been woven and worn in pairs. Kashmir's climate encouraged the development of a warm, supple accessory. Two other factors were also important advantages: the supply of fine wool available and the clean, soft water of Lake Srinagar.

The wool in question comes from a mountain goat, *Capra hircus*, which lives at altitude. In the cold winter months, it produces a fine down on its belly which it sheds in springtime on the mountain thorn bushes. The down or *pashm* is only produced at high altitude. It was so prized in Europe that, in the 17th century, merchants decided to send goats back to Europe to produce cashmere wool. Unfortunately, the ship carrying all the female goats was lost at sea and only a handful of the male goats survived the arduous journey – these goats did not again encounter

sub-zero temperatures and so never again produced the fine *pashmina* down.

Pure *pashmina* is still harvested in the traditional way, although its popularity today has led to many imitations and mixtures. The wool is sorted into various qualities and then spun. The finest wool is cream in colour and is generally used in its natural state, although it can also be dyed in light colours. This finest quality is known as *tush* or *shah tus*, and is the wool used for "ring shawls", which are so fine that they can be pulled through a wedding ring. There is a ban on exporting modern *pashmina* from India, designed to protect dwindling stocks from the unscrupulous – purchasing an antique *pashmina* avoids these ethical issues, and such shawls are usually much finer than the modern equivalent.

Kashmir shawls can be woven or embroidered. The embroidered shawls were produced alongside the woven shawls as a quicker and therefore cheaper way of manufacturing. Patterns for woven and embroidered shawls are virtually interchangeable. However, there are some very attractive embroidered stoles

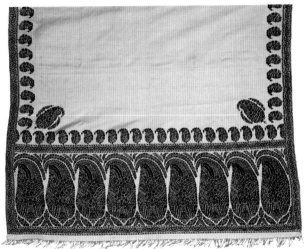

▲ **Indian shawl**
Of *pashmina* wool, woven with mosaic upright *boteh*
characteristic of 1815–25. Such shawls were often worn
by European ladies over their muslin evening gowns.
£4,000–6,000/$6,400–9,600

◀ **Shawl with saffron ground**
An attractive Indian shawl with an unusual ground which will
increase its value to collectors signed on the reverse, from
around 1815–20.
£1,000–1,500/$1,600–2,400

worked on net and fine wools from the Delhi area which are worthy of note. Woven Kashmir shawls are always woven using the tapestry technique (*see* p.11), and a fine shawl could take two weavers two or three years to complete. Contemporary European shawls were woven on a drawloom, rather than hand-woven. It is therefore always possible to tell an Indian shawl from a European shawl. The former will not look tidy on the reverse, with threads running in all directions joining small areas of colour, unlike the neat reverses of European shawls, with threads running left to right, from selvedge to selvedge.

Common motifs for 17th-century shawls are elegantly drawn and extremely accurate botanical representations of poppies, roses, marigolds, and sometimes cyprus trees, all usually in red, blue, yellow or green on an ivory ground. Less common are saffron yellow, red or dark blue grounds. The depth of the *pallu* – the deep border at either end of the shawl – is approximately 20–30 cm (8–12in), containing motifs which are sometimes tiny and arranged

in rows, and sometimes single flower sprays. Mosaic flowerheads became popular in the mid- to late 17th century and continued to be used in modified form throughout the 18th century. The size of the motifs decreased during the course of the century, until tiny bud motifs filled the *pallu*.

It is said that the Indian shawl came to Europe with Napoleon's soldiers returning from the Egyptian campaigns – by the end of the 18th century, fashionable European ladies were clamouring for "cachemire" shawls to drape around their shoulders over the Empire-line fashions of the day. They were fantastically expensive, costing similar amounts to diamonds and pearls. The Empress Josephine was a devoted wearer of these shawls and is said to have bought such a large number that her husband, Napoleon, was forced to step in to curtail her expenditure. One of the earliest portraits of a fashionable lady wearing a shawl is thought to be Jacques-Louis David's 1790 portrait of the Marquise de Sorcy de Thelusson, now in the Alte Pinakotek, Munich.

◀ **Kashmir shawl**
An excellent example of high-quality weaving by Indian craftsmen following a French design. The ivory centre with invading fronds and the upright cones at each end are classically French in tone, as this shawl was probably destined for export to France.
£1,500–3,000/$2,400–4,800

▶ *Rumal* **shawl with grid centre**
A square *rumal* shawl with unusual grid centre – this rare design adds to the value of the piece which dates from the 1850s.
£1,000–1,500/$1,600–2,400

# 19th-Century Indian Shawls

By the beginning of the 19th century, Kashmir was struggling to keep up with demand from Europe for their shawls. This led to a technical change in production. When, in 1831, Victor Jacquemont visited Kashmir on a survey mission for the *Jardin du Roi*, later the Natural History Museum in Paris, he noted that shawls were being produced in small fragments and being sewn together like patchwork. Formerly they had been woven in one, or possibly two, pieces.

This new procedure speeded up production, as well as satisfying the requirements of the tax authorities at the time. A weaver was never allowed to have more than a few inches of shawl on his loom untaxed. The owner's agents would inspect the looms regularly and cut shawl cloth from the loom to have it stamped and taxed, rather than wait over a year for the completion of the shawl. A patchwork shawl can therefore be dated to the 19th century, whereas one woven in a single piece is likely to date from the beginning of the 19th century or earlier.

Shawls in the Indian technique were not only produced in Kashmir itself. In 1810 a number of shawl weavers left Kashmir to avoid extortionate taxation demands, and set up their looms further south in the Punjab and Lahore. Although these weavers made use of the same wools and looms, the quality of the shawls seems to be inferior to Kashmir shawls. This was generally attributed to the particularly high quality of the water in Kashmir.

Further migrations caused by famine and by epidemics of cholera followed in 1833, when the wool used also changed to merino sheep wool rather than cashmere. A further wave of emigration followed to Kirman in Persia, where shawl cloth was produced in quantity for the Qajar empire. This shawl cloth was also woven with merino wool, which is thicker and glossier than cashmere. Many panels of shawl cloth survive with Persian gilt embroidery, sometimes with seed pearls as treasured family heirlooms. They are known in Farsi as *termeh*.

**◀ "Dolman" coat or cape**
Recycled from an unfashionable Indian shawl into a stylish mantle with sloping "dolman" sleeves in the 1870s – shops such as "A la ville de Bombay" in Paris specialized in remodelling shawls in this manner. £600–800/$1,000–1,300

**▼ *Rumal* shawl with figures**
An extremely fine patchwork shawl in the *rumal* style, filled with tiny figures, dating from the 1850s. £800–1,500/$1,300–2,400

**▶ *Rumal* shawl**
The black-and-white outlines used in this patchwork shawl are typical of the 1860s. £500–£1,000/ $800–1,600

The common shape of shawls before 1800 – a plain field with a deep border of *boteh* (cones) at either end on ivory ground – began to alter. By 1800, motifs had increased in size, with large, upright, floral mosaic *boteh* filling the *pallus*. These *boteh* can be 30cm (11¾in) tall. The ground colours can vary through saffron, blue and red. By 1815, the *boteh* are tipping slightly and the space between them is filling with flowers, and by 1825 they are outlined only by a narrow band of plain ground and are definitely slanting. Sometimes, the gallery of smaller *boteh* above the main *pallu* slants in the opposite direction.

Square shawls had always been produced alongside long shawls, but these had generally only been "Moon shawls" (*see* p.105). From the 1840s onwards, square shawls with patterns very similar to long shawls, that is to say filled with undulating vines, *boteh* and flowers, were popular both in India and Europe. They are known as *rumal* shawls, which means handkerchief, referring to their shape.

By 1840, the shawl trade with Europe was well established and European designs start to appear in India. The plain field gradually shrinks, and in the 1860s only a small residual medallion remains. Pattern, with huge, snaking *boteh,* now fills the whole shawl. Colours are lush, with duck-egg blue, raspberry pink and scarlet established as new favourites. Aniline dyes become available in the late 1850s, especially "Perkins purple", a strong mauve. The presence of this mauve will always indicate an origin after 1856. Other non-vegetable dyes appear around this time which are harsher, brighter and more prone to fading.

By 1870 the European lady was wearing dresses with bustles and no longer required a shawl. For a time, she might have her now unfashionable shawl converted into a flowing cape or mantle, and in Paris there were a number of shops which specialized in this process. However, eventually this change in fashion spelled the death knell for both the Kashmir and the European shawl industries.

▲ **Shawl with yellow ground**
A fine shawl of the 1840s with an unusual egg-yolk yellow ground. This rare colour will increase the value over shawls with more common black or white grounds. **£400–500/$640–800**

# French Shawls

The French shawl industry was set up in response to the huge demand for Indian shawls from Kashmir at the end of the 18th century. The demand was for Indian design, on fine, supple wool as close as possible to Indian *pashmina* wool. This sometimes meant silk was used, sometimes wool.

The superfine shawl in ivory with blue and pink floral cones at either end was a perfect answer to a fashion dilemma: what to wear over a wafer-thin transparent muslin dress of the Empire style and be both warm and elegant. When one considers that the faster young ladies were known to dampen their muslin in order to make it even more figure-hugging, the popularity of the shawl becomes understandable.

The French silk industry was already very sophisticated and could respond quickly to the demand. The main centres of shawl production were those of the silk industry – Paris and Lyons – with subsidiary factories in other parts of France. At first, shawls were closely modelled on their Indian counterparts and can

only be differentiated by looking at the back of the shawl, where the European draw loom technique looks quite different to the Indian hand tapestry weave.

France was increasingly conscious of its place in the international market, and in the 1830s staged a series of *Expositions Universelles*, designed to showcase French manufacture and design. Shawls by leading designers took an important place at these exhibitions. They produced shawls with varied and sophisticated motifs, and darker grounds such as mustard yellow, sage green and dark blue. With the new puffed sleeves, smaller, square shawls became fashionable.

A notable manufacturer specializing in non-Indian shawl designs was Guillaume Ternaux (1763–1833) who received a commission from Napoleon to produce shawls for the Empress Marie Louise. He produced shawls with motifs of naturalistic European flowers, some designed by the artist Jean-Baptiste Isabey. Very few survive, although two have recently been traced to his descendants and exhibited.

**◄ Shawl in the style of Anthony Berrus**
A dramatic shawl from 1845–50 with three-dimensional effect.
This kind of design, which pushes the design out and into the
borders, is typically French and particularly associated with the
designer Anthony Berrus. £500–1,000/$800–1,600

# Collecting Signatures

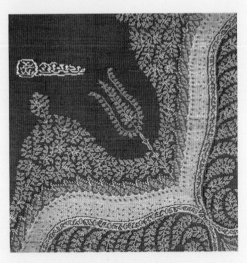

**▲ Signature of Nicholas Frédéric Hébert**
A capital H can just be made out in the circle on the left.
The remaining signature is a pseudo-Arabic version of
"cachemir pur". £700–1,000/$1,200–1,600

**▲ Shawl with sailing barques**
An unusual shawl from the 1840s featuring a black ground,
and woven with sailing barques at each corner. Any such
pictorial element will ensure increased interest from collectors.
£700–1,000/$1,200–1,600

The fashions of the 1840s saw a more natural waist level and the beginning of fuller skirts, leading to the introduction of the crinoline, originally a horsehair petticoat (from the French *crin*, for horsehair). Both square and long shawls continued to be worn, and over the next two decades skirts became increasingly full. Their size prevented ladies from wearing a coat, with the result that the shawl became a very important accessory. The shape of these shawls became almost exclusively rectangular, with patterns filling almost the entire area. Burgundy red was an especially popular colour.

Fashion dealt the shawl industry a terrible blow in the 1870s. The fashionable lady abandoned her crinoline, and donned the bustle. Dresses were tailored and shaped to the figure. The last thing such a lady required was a voluminous shawl to obscure her figure. The result was a dramatic decline in the popularity of shawls and the total collapse of the shawl industry, from which it never recovered.

Almost all signed shawls are French in their origin. The practice arose out of the French manufacturers' concerns about sub-standard shawls which still bore the name "cachemire". As a result, they added signatures to their shawls as a sign of guaranteed quality.

A signature woven into a shawl will increase its desirability considerably. In addition to the woven signatures, shawls were originally labelled with a silk circular woven disc, giving the medals won by the manufacturer at various world fairs. These, of course, can provide an additional way of dating a shawl.

Some of the best-known initials and signatures, found in the four corners of the shawl, are: *Gen Ainé & Cie* (Gaussen Ainé et Cie), *FM* (Fortier & Maillard), *LF* (Lion Frères around 1852), and *JC* (Joseph Chanel in the 1860s).

Fortier & Maillard also signed their name in pseudo-Arabic script in the central field of the shawl, as did Nicholas Frédéric Hébert (*see* above) and his son Emile, who succeeded him in 1855. The leading manufacturer Laurence Biètry (*see* p.104) wove or embroidered his name or the word "cachemire" into his shawls. On special commissions, he is known to have woven in the coat of arms of the purchaser.

**▲ Square shawl**
A typical square shape from the 1860s, when the shawl industry was already in decline – double-sided shawls were also introduced at the time in order to reawaken the interest of customers.
£300–600/$500–1,000

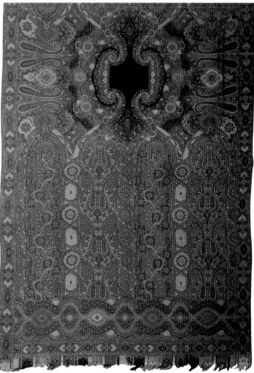

# British and Austrian Shawls

The mania for Kashmir shawls was widespread throughout Europe. Apart from France, the main European centres of production of woven shawls were Paisley and Edinburgh in Scotland, Norwich in England and Vienna in Austria.

The most important feature of the Indian shawl was the softness of the wool, which was difficult to imitate successfully. An obvious solution to the problem was to buy Kashmir wool on the open market, but the various trade embargoes on the import of foreign goods prevented this.

Manufacturers experimented with silks, and with silk and wool mixtures. The most common solution was to use a fine silk warp and either a silk weft with wool brocade weft, or an all-wool weft. Norwich had a considerable technical advantage in that they had been weaving half-silks for generations. Edinburgh was set up for damask-weaving. However, by the early 19th century the differences had evened out and all centres were using a draw loom. In the 1820s the introduction of the Jacquard loom speeded up production and allowed a greater complexity of pattern.

Imitating Indian patterns was a particular strength of the French shawl manufacturers, who employed designers as a matter of course. Edinburgh shawl manufacturers such as Gibb & MacDonald made regular trips to France to study shawls and to purchase designs, as did Norwich and Paisley shawl manufacturers. However, the lack of emphasis on design is probably a defining feature when comparing French shawls with their competition.

The beginnings of the Paisley shawl industry are not clear, but by 1812 it was reported that over a hundred looms were employed in the town. Workshops of four to six looms encouraged debate and exchange of ideas; the weavers were supporters of the Chartist movement and had their own trade union. With the introduction of the Jacquard loom came mass production in large factories – Paisley in the 1830s was almost entirely dependent on the shawl industry and therefore on the whim of fashion, while the name of Paisley was all but synonymous in the Victorian mind with shawls, and in particular with the patterns they bore. When fashions changed, the

▼ **Shawl with architectural designs**

A finely woven shawl, with architectural designs on an orange ground, in a manner typical of the 1850s. Despite the fine working, such shawls are worth far less than Indian equivalents.
£400–600/$640–1,000

▲ **Black-ground shawl**

An unusual shawl with a black ground – such sombre colours are typical of the 1850s. During the 1850s and 60s, the highly-skilled dyers at Paisley were starting to use aniline dyes rather than natural substances.
£500–800/$1000–1500

industry was badly hit, and in 1842 the town was declared bankrupt. With the personal encouragement of Queen Victoria, the industry had recovered enough to be cited for quality at the Great Exhibition of 1851. A diversity of shawls were produced, using materials that included fur, angora damask and silk. Rumours abounded of Paisley weavers copying French patterns, with the result that it is sometimes difficult to identify a shawl as French or Scottish unless it is signed.

Edinburgh, too, was an important centre of production in the early 19th century, but failed to adapt to new trends and by the 1830s was no longer a name to conjure with, although individual manufacturers continued. One such was David Sime, who closed his factory in 1853. His career has been of great use to shawl historians as he deposed patents for his shawl patterns from 1843 to 1847.

The Norwich shawl-weaving industry enjoyed the royal patronage of Queen Charlotte. High-quality shawls were produced by companies such as Clabburn, Son & Crisp, whose rich, ribbed silk shawls frequently appear on the market, where they are much appreciated. A particular pillar-box red in wool is a favourite Norwich ground colour. Raspberry pink silk grounds are also often cited as "Norwich Pink". Superb printed-silk gauze shawls by Towler & Campin are also characteristically Norwich, often produced on a black ground.

The Austrian shawl-weaving industry developed parallel to and in overt competition with the Scottish and French industries. A collection of sample cards made for the Emperor Francis I in 1807 provides rare documentary evidence of Austrian shawl-weaving. Beginning with plain shawls with attached woven borders, it progressed to patterned shawls in the 1820s. By the 1830s, over 4,000 looms were in use.

Austria exported large numbers of shawls to Germany, Italy, Turkey, Russia and Poland, and even to North America. To the collector, a documented Austrian shawl would be very interesting. However, without documents, it is difficult to tell an Austrian shawl from its other European counterparts. The use of metal thread, however, in a mid-19th century shawl may well signify an Austrian manufacture.

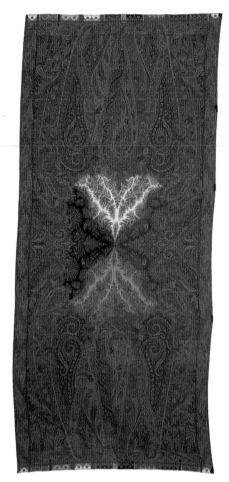

**▲ Norwich shawl**
A square shawl of fine ivory wool with naturalistic flower sprays,
woven by Towler & Campin in 1845. **£400–600/$640–1,000**

**◄ "Four Seasons" shawl**
So-called because the centre is divided into contrasting quarters – this
shawl from 1845 is thought to be designed by the famous French shawl
designer Anthony Berrus. **£700–1,200/$1,200–2,000**

# Signed and Exhibition Shawls

It is safe to say that, with very few exceptions, a signed shawl is likely to be of French origin. French manufacturers started signing their limited editions of shawls as a method of protecting individual weavers' reputations. A signature was a guarantee of the manufacturer of quality or of the fact that they were made of genuine Kashmir wool, and not a cheaper imitation. The movement to sign shawls was led by Laurence Biètry, a Parisian manufacturer and president of the *Conseil des Prud'hommes de la Seine*, a body which registered designs. He published a pamphlet in 1848 urging the use of signatures, or at least the attachment of labels to the reverse.

The importance of the *Expositions Universelles*, the equivalent of the English trade fairs of the 19th century, cannot be overemphasized. Signed shawls were important exhibits. As early as 1834, the weaver Gaussen Aîné & Cie exhibited a shawl entitled *Isphahan* designed by Amadée Couder (*see* above right). It was woven with exotic pavilions and

cartouches with Arabic calligraphy, giving the name of the weaver, the designer, the date and the title. Gaussen and Couder followed up this success in 1839 with the shawl entitled *Nou Rouz*, or "New Year", which won a gold medal.

The second important manufacturer to sign and exhibit was the company of Duché. Founded in 1841 by the brothers Théophile, François and Adolphe, with other members of their family, it continued in various forms until the 1860s when key members died. Their records are incomplete, as the designs they registered from 1836 onwards were destroyed when the patent expired, leaving only the text record. Two shawls have been identified as theirs from this record, *Le Phénix* and *Le Jupiter*. Both shawls are of the highest quality of design and weaving and have their title woven cunningly into the design. Other important names of this time are Fortier & Maillard, well known for their striped shawls, and Nicholas Frédéric Hébert, famous for technical innovation.

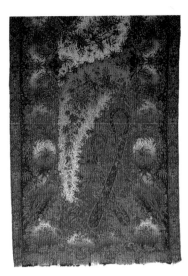

**▶ Duché Ainé shawl**
An outstanding shawl of the 1840s, with the firm's name woven into the corners. The subtle gradation of colour is achieved by pre-dying the warp threads.
£12,000–14,000/$19,200–20,400

**◀ Isphahan shawl**
Designed by Amadée Couder, and woven by Gaussen for the 1836 Paris *Exposition Universelle* trade fair.
£1,000–5,000/$1,600–8,000 depending on condition and colour

# Collecting
# *Moon Shawls*

**▲ A brightly coloured saffron moon shawl**
In this shawl of *c.*1840 from Nîmes, France, the moon and quarters are woven with an ivory ground which contrasts dramatically with the yellow. £1,500–2,000/$2,400–3,200

There are many collectors of these charming square shawls. The central medallion is said to represent the moon, and the four quarter-medallions, one at each corner, are the four quarters of the moon's cycle. The tradition goes back at least to the 18th century in India. This Indian form was introduced to Europe around 1800 and in time was also produced in Europe.

Indian moon shawls of the 18th century are woven with similar devices to long shawls. However, there are some patterns peculiar to the moon shawl. One features stripes woven with spot motifs. The stripes pass through the medal-lions as if transparent. Favourite colours for this variant are red, blue and white. Sometimes the spot motifs are tiny birds. A chequerboard of brightly coloured squares, each with a sprig flower, is also popular, with a particularly deep indigo blue as the dominant colour.

In Europe, the fashion for moon shawls reached its height between 1820 and 1840, when sleeves were large and puffed, and a square shawl folded on the diagonal fitted perfectly over the shoulders. Some of the greatest French designers produced moon shawls *"à l'indienne"*. The fashion continued in continental Europe for several decades after high fashion had adopted other shapes, as part of traditional folk costume.

The most important partnership to produce signed and especially exhibition shawls is that of the designer Anthony Berrus and the manufacturer Laurence Biètry, who had lead the movement to sign shawls. In 1847 the first designs for square shawls appeared, and in 1849 at least five *à pivot* designs (on a diagonal axis) were exhibited. Architectural motifs moved to the forefront by 1851, and drapery makes an appearance in 1862 along with Greek key patterns.

After 1855, Bourgois Frères, Joseph Chanel and Gérard & Cantigny all wove Berrus designs. However, since Berrus employed up to two hundred designers over a period of forty years, his firm's designs were certainly bought by many other manufacturers.

Anthony Berrus continued to work until 1873, producing designs which were never to be woven. He has left a record of his work in the form of books of designs, most now in the Musée des Arts Décoratifs in Paris. They are a unique record of a prolific artist, and of great interest to the shawl historian.

▼ **Printed shawl**
Woven in 1843 with alternating rows of cones.
Even high-quality printed shawls are valued less than
woven shawls by collectors. **£150–250/$250–400**

▲ **Light printed shawl**
A typical shawl of *c.*1850 in light fabric which matched the
voluminous dresses of the time. A rare survivor as the ground is
so thin, but still relatively inexpensive. **£150–200/$250–320**

▶ **Canton shawl**
An ivory Canton shawl made for the Spanish market.
This example has unusual fern motifs in place of
pagodas and flowers. **£200–400/$320–640**

# Printed and Canton Shawls

Printed shawls were produced by many manufacturers alongside woven shawls. Woven shawls were more expensive and aimed at the middle and upper classes, whereas printed shawls were designed for everyday wear, although there are exceptions to this rule. Paisley, for example, printed shawls of fine quality on the silk gauzes for which they were famous. These Paisley shawls were expensive and classed as luxury goods, and Norwich also produced fine gauze shawls.

Documentary history of the printed shawl industry is patchy, although Paisley has three pattern books from the firm of Todd Shortridge & Co. in Dumbarton recording the period from 1785 to 1802.

Early shawls were printed using large, carved wooden blocks. Each colour was applied separately, so that a complicated pattern might require twenty or more blocks to complete a repeat. Later shawl-printing blocks used inserted copper wires in blocks approximately 31cm (12in) square. By the time shawls had declined in popularity in the third quarter of the 19th century, roller printing had been adopted. The

quality of printing, therefore, declined along with the popularity of the shawl itself.

To the collector, condition and documentary provenance are key factors in determining both price and desirability. Shawls of the early 19th century are very much in the Indian mode, with small sprig patterns covering light-coloured grounds. They are quite inexpensive and make wonderful collectors' objects and gifts. Shawls produced in the mid-19th century tend to be square and have brightly coloured grounds and larger patterns.

A large part of the production of printed shawls was destined for Europe and the conservative regional populations, for whom a shawl was not a fashion item so much as a necessity. A good square 'kerchief shawl formed part of folk costume, particularly the bride's wear, for much of the 19th and early 20th centuries.

By the mid-1840s, superfine wool gauze shawls appeared. They were of very high quality and very attractive. Many had silk ribbons woven into the ground. These shawls are very rarely found in good

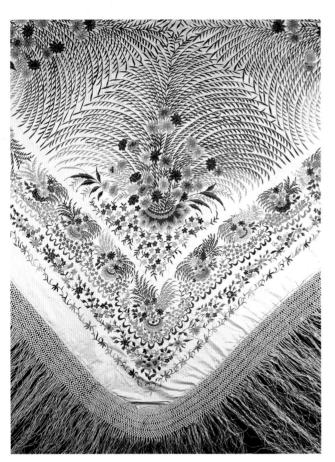

condition. If the moths haven't feasted on them, the silk and wool in the mixture have reacted with each other. The wool, being acid, will eventually rot the silk, given a significant exposure to light. A shawl in good condition, of printed woollen gauze, also known as challis, is therefore a rare item.

However, the more substantial printed woollen shawls of the 1850s and 60s are also very attractive. They are sometimes printed to shape, in the form of large semi-circular capes. If you are lucky enough to find a printed shawl with details of where it was printed and by whom, you can treble the value compared to an identical shawl without a provenance.

The term "Canton shawl" indicates the nationality of the maker rather than the country of origin. They are also known as "Spanish shawls" after the country of destination, and even "Manilla shawls" after the town where they were embroidered. These shawls were produced in Manilla at the beginning of the 19th century and continued to be produced well into the 20th century, forming part of the trade from the new

world to the old. They were sold by Liberty's in London, often in their original box, and graced many a piano in 1920s London.

They are remarkably uniform in size, being usually 153cm (5ft) square and edged with a deep silk fringe approximately 61cm (2ft) long, which can be of contrasting colour to the shawl centre. The centres are made of *crêpe de chine* – a Chinese silk – and can be all colours of the rainbow, but the most common colours are black and white. Ivory shawls embroidered with ivory silks are the most popular at auction today.

The embroidery is entirely double-sided, and was worked by two embroiderers working at each side of a shawl mounted on a frame. The needle would be pushed through by one worker and taken up by the other. In this way, seamless floral patterns appear. Pagodas are a favourite theme, with courtiers in gardens another. Very rarely, a more technological subject matter is approached – I have seen one red shawl embroidered in white with a procession of aeroplanes, trains, cars and motorcycles.

# Printed Textiles

## From the 17th century on: exotic quilts, chintzes, muslins and designer headscarves

▲ **Indian** *palampore*
A superb Indian printed and quilted chintz cover or *palampore*, painted with large blooms on a tree of life, made for the Dutch market in the 1720s. **£33,000–35,000/$53,000–56,000**

The word "chintz" is thought to be a corruption of *chitta* or spotted cloth. This suggestion is backed up by the Portuguese use of the term *pintado* or "spotted cloth" for chintzes. It is one of many Indian terms in current use in the English textile vocabulary, for example khaki, shawl, pyjama and calico, to name but a few.

The history of the Indian printed-cotton industry is complex. India has a long tradition of printing cottons and also of exporting them. Some of the earliest known dyed cottons have been excavated from burial grounds at Fostat outside Cairo, exported there from India as early as the 14th century and perhaps even earlier.

They have always been popular on the European market. The East India Companies of both England and Holland were responsible for introducing chintzes into Europe in the early 17th century as part of the cargo of valuable spices returning from the Spice Islands. At this time, Europe was only able to produce fugitive printed textiles which ran in water. Their life was therefore limited. Indian prints were colourfast and were commonly thought to renew themselves when dipped in water. This must have seemed miraculous to 17th-century buyers.

Although Europeans were appreciative of the qualities of these cottons, the East India Company did not seize the opportunity of trading them until the middle of the 16th century. It was at this point that the board of the East India Company is first known to have suggested that instead of the red ground favoured by Indian customers, the cotton painters and printers might like to consider sending white-ground chintzes for sale in England.

This was the beginning of a long and profitable exchange of ideas between Europe and India. Indeed, over the centuries, it becomes

◀ **Lady's robe**

A lady's robe of fine linen from *c.* 1785, appliquéd with chintz flowers in the *broderie perse* technique. **£2,000–4,000/$3,200–6,400**

▲ ***Palampore* hanging**

Made in India for the European market, this hanging lacks its border and is therefore quite inexpensive. The palm tree on the left is typical of the late 18th century. **£800–1,500/$1,300–2,400**

increasingly difficult to tell who is influencing whom. English patterns were sent to India, so that a more acceptable product returned for sale. However, patterns of European flowers returned to England as wildly exotic blooms when interpreted by Indian draftsmen. The hybrids, part English, part Indian, were an enormous success.

By the mid-17th century, chintzes were being commissioned by English manufacturers to appeal specifically to the aristocratic élite. Bedcovers, quilts and wall-hangings began to reach England and were well received by the *cognoscenti*, eager for novelty. It is these luxury goods rather than the sprigged dress fabrics that were the first exports to Europe which have survived. This is probably due to the fact that the initial expense of a large-scale painted textile encouraged owners to preserve it long after the dresses of the day had been worn out.

The main channel for ordering chintzes was through company agents in western and northern India. The main areas of production were Suronj, Ahmedabad, and Bhuranpur. After 1680, orders to western India fell off and were redirected to the Coromandel coast. Production increased in the next decade, and European printers became anxious about their livelihoods. France tried to ban the import of foreign printed textiles in 1686, and England followed suit in 1701 and 1720. We can judge how successful these bans were by the fact that the majority of chintzes in our possession today date from the time of prohibition.

Collectors should pay particular attention to the reverse of quilts and hangings in case the East India Company stamp is still present, allowing accurate dating. It is also interesting to note that some Indian printed hangings are made from European linen exported to India rather than the usual fine Indian cotton.

► **Printed and painted** *palampore*
Made in India for the European market.
This example from the late 18th
century is in a fragile condition.
£500–1,000/$800–1,600

▲ *Kalimkari* **prayer arch**
This 19th-century Persian prayer
arch is printed and painted with
cypress trees, emblematic of faith,
and also has peacocks and tigers at
its base. £400–600/$640–1,000

◄ **Detail of block-printed cotton**
This cotton is typical of the fabric used for lining
costumes or hangings, and was used to back
an 18th-century embroidered prayer mat.
£50–100/$80–160

# Chintzes, *Kalimkari* and Printed Cottons

The surviving body of Indian printed cottons is largely composed of furnishing fabrics. A large proportion are in the form of wall-hangings or bed-covers featuring a flowering tree, usually on a rocky mound, with birds among the branches. These are known by their Indian name of *palampores*.

They evolved for export to Europe, and can be quilted in contemporary European style. The larger the designs, the earlier the chintz is likely to be, while a *palampore* chintz with a more elaborate ground probably dates from the latter part of the 18th century or even 19th century.

Colours in early 18th-century chintzes tend to be simple, with strong reds, blues and yellows. Green is produced by overdying indigo with yellow. As the use of large blocks of colour begins to die out with the passing of large flower patterns, it seems to the naked eye as if the colours are murkier.

Alongside the production of such luxury printed textiles, India was also exporting a range of block-printed and painted cottons of varying quality. Because of the influence of the various East India Companies who supplied European printed cottons on which to base their designs, Indian production was extraordinarily sensitive to European markets. These European samples were used to produce chintzes, and also pieces known as "Trade embroideries". The export chintzes of the 18th and 19th centuries are well worth studying and collecting.

A second type of chintz was being produced at the same time for more local religious demand. Muslim needs were being met for prayer arches, usually in a simple red and blue palette, based on a niche with a central cypress tree. Persia was producing similar textiles called *kalimkari* (literally "penwork") for domestic use. It is very difficult to tell them apart except occasionally by iconography. The majority of those surviving are from the 19th and early 20th centuries.

For Hindu markets, chintzes with narrative patterns were produced with didactic purposes. The

**▲ Detail of block-printed cotton**
This high-quality 18th-century Indian print was designed for the European market, and was probably intended as a bed hanging or wall covering. £400–1,000/$640–1,600

Armenian merchant community also commissioned chintzes with Christian iconography for their churches both in India and abroad. There are splendid Indian chintzes of the 17th and 18th centuries hanging in Jerusalem churches, for example.

Supplying less specific needs for serviceable printed cottons, there was also a lively industry both in Persia and India for block-printed cottons. Fragments of 18th- and 19th-century Indian block prints are available for small sums and can be exquisite. The majority of 19th-century block prints are very affordable. Typically they feature a simple floral *boteh* against a plain ground. Persian examples tend to be confined to red and blue tones, whereas Indian palettes are wider and can feature gilt highlights.

By the middle of the 19th century, Indian printed cottons were struggling to compete with European imports. However, in the 20th century, they were again able to compete and today are still dominant in certain sectors such as dress and furnishing cottons.

# Collecting Mezzara

**▲ Mezzara, Italian, 1840s**
Fashionable Italian ladies wrapped themselves in these colourful Indian-inspired cottons as a kind of opera cloak. £400–1,000/$640–1,600

Mezzara is a printed and painted cotton hanging of roughly the size of a large double bed. They were produced in the 19th century in Italy, particularly in Genoa. Despite their size, they are thought to have been worn around the shoulders by fine ladies as a kind of evening cloak. When the crowds of theatre-goers flooded down the steps of the opera house, the austere black and white of the gentlemen's tuxedos would have been set off by the voluminous folds of the mezzara around their ladies' shoulders.

Their design is based on Indian painted bedspreads or *palampores* of the 18th and 19th centuries, with the white cotton ground usually painted with an elaborate flowering tree, exotic blooms and animals. The cotton of an Italian mezzara is usually of a coarser quality and looser weave than than that of its Indian counterpart, and the colours used are usually limited to red, blue and black rather than the wider palette of the Indian printmakers, which included green and yellow, as well as gold. The types of flowers depicted can also betray their Italian origins.

The collector can find examples of these Italian chintzes at a fraction of the price of a contemporary Indian chintz, and, with their attractive designs, they are well worth collecting.

**▲ Detail of a printed cotton**
This typically roller-printed English furnishing cotton from 1825 shows a *trompe l'oeil* window opening on to a garden.
£1,000–1,500/$1,600–2,400

**► Muslin dress**
A dress of diaphanous ivory muslin from the 1860s printed with bands of flowers.
£300–500/$480–800

# 19th-Century English Printed Cottons

While the main inventions in the production of printing cotton in England occurred in the 18th century, it was not until the 19th century that they were extensively used and the industry developed.

Printing cotton was banned in England until 1774 and heavy excise duties were not lifted until 1831. In an act of 1774, lasting until 1811, three blue threads were woven into the selvedge of the new British all-cotton cloth to distinguish it from French cloth, allowing the printer to claim a lower excise rate. Some British firms, however, printed on Indian imported calico that did not therefore have blue threads.

The centre of the printing industry had previously been in London along the Thames, water being necessary for the printing process. After 1774, the focus gradually moved to Lancashire, and centred on Manchester. The area was ideal, being close to the weaving centres of cotton cloth, and served by the docks at Liverpool for exporting pieces, especially to America. By 1820, most cotton printing was carried out there, leaving London with only a few specialist printers for items such as pocket handkerchiefs.

Bromley Hall, Preston, led the field in the early 19th century, producing high-quality wood block prints which are highly sought after by collectors today. In the period from 1800 to 1810, there was a fashion for "drab" style prints, generally featuring colours such as brown, olive and yellow. In 1805, there was also a short fashion for exotic patterns such as "Indian" flowers on a red ground, chinoiserie scenes, Egyptian motifs and also neo-classical designs in Pompeian colours, that is with bold, often primary, contrasts. After 1815, palm trees and game birds were increasingly depicted, and these remained in fashion for about ten years.

The 1820s saw more formal patterns introduced, including stripes, and from 1825 to 1830, floral trails with fern-like foliage. From 1800 to 1818 pillar prints were also popular, often combining birds and floral patterns. They were revived in 1825 in the newly developed mineral colours, and were popular into the 1830s. "Rainbowing" also made use of this advance in the 1820s and 30s, where stripes of bright colours were blended at the edges.

◄ **Printed cotton dress**
A cotton day dress of striped printed cotton from the 1830s.
The outsize balloon sleeves are known as "imbecile sleeves".
£300–500/$500–800

▲ **Detail of chintz**
A chintz produced by Bromley Hall in the 1760s, with a typical blue and white design
of birds and foliage. **£500–600/$800–900** per metre (39½in)

Roller printing was patented in the late 18th century, but the limited circumference of the roller meant it was not developed until after 1815 in Lancashire, when repeat patterns were small enough to fit on rollers. Early roller prints often depict sporting and rustic scenes in monochrome red, black or sepia, as it was too difficult to apply multiple colours. They usually have a slightly strange appearance, with elongated horizontals and squashed verticals, reflecting the shape of the roller. There were also floral designs, printed the other way round, so a pattern developed with continuous parallel vertical cascades of flowers.

By the 1830s, perhaps reflecting interest in the Gothic and in romanticism, "fancy machine grounds" were popular. These are where any exposed ground not covered by the primary design is also patterned, often in a diaper pattern. Gothic windows were used as inspiration along with other *trompe l'oeil* devices such as imitation woven silks, needlework and other architectural details. There was also a fashion for exotic birds and butterflies, prompted by the publication of Audubon's *The Birds of America* in 1827–38.

One of the main innovations of the first half of the 19th century was in dyeing technology. Until 1810, all printing was based on vegetable dyes, but after this a new colour palette was introduced, based on mineral colours, transforming the 18th-century palette, and producing new colours such as manganese brown, chrome yellow and a solid green. The development of synthetic dyes continued throughout the 19th century, leading to new colours with which to print the increasing volume of designs. With the mechanization of the cotton-printing industry in the mid-19th century, cotton prints gained a wide appeal to consumers across classes. The second half of the century sees a divergence between mass-produced printed cottons and hand-crafted pieces for the luxury end of the market.

Cotton is not a very durable fabric, and suffers also from its utilitarian nature, which results in cotton items being used until worn out. Today, the pieces most sought after by collectors are those dating from before mass production. However, later high-quality pieces in a good condition are becoming collectable.

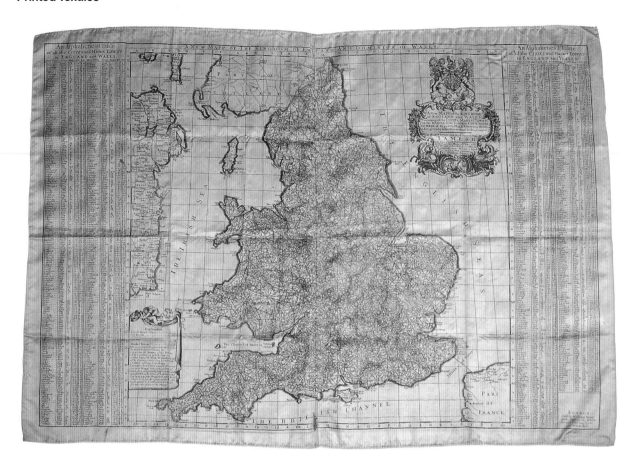

# Printed Handkerchiefs

Printed handkerchiefs are an interesting field for textile collectors and are often sought after by collectors of other subjects too, depending on what they depict, for example maps or cartoons. Until the end of the 19th century, they represented an important way to commemorate events and disseminate information. They could also be used in a subversive way, the true political feelings of the owner being shown by the handkerchief in his pocket – a known French handkerchief of 1818, for example, is a statement of Royalist triumph at the defeat of Napoleon.

One of the earliest printed handkerchiefs to survive dates from the late 17th century and is held in the Victoria & Albert Museum, London. It is printed on satin and depicts a map of England and Wales. Copperplate printing was introduced into England from Ireland in 1756, and was used for handkerchiefs into the 19th century, even after it fell out of more general usage with technological advances in block printing and then roller printing. The engraved plates of the copperplate technique lent themselves to the illustrative character needed to print handkerchiefs.

Handkerchief printing in England was centred on London, even after the main cotton-printing industry moved from the Thames area to Lancashire in the late 18th century. Normandy and Alsace in France were also noted for their handkerchiefs, producing small plate-printed handkerchiefs as well as larger printed headsquares. The early examples, up until the mid-19th century, are generally monochrome, as it was too difficult to apply multiple colours using the available printing technology. Even by the mid-19th century, there are commonly only two colours against the ground, for example black, red and white, but later in the century, with the advance in technology, more complex colour combinations could be used.

It is usually the date and subject of a handkerchief that determine its value. Early royal commemorative handkerchiefs are much sought after, such as "The Reign of George III", from 1811, which records dates and events from his reign. Famous battles were commemorated too, such as Waterloo and the victories of the Crimean War. Pieces connected with the French Revolution are rare, and highly desirable.

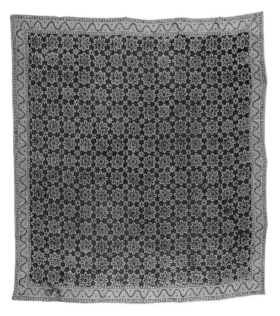

**▲ Indian handkerchief**
Printed in Bengal on fine cotton for the European market
early in the 19th century. £300–600/$500–1,000

**◄ English handkerchief**
One of the earliest surviving printed handkerchiefs, dating
from the late 17th century, printed on silk with a map of
England and Wales. £2,000–4,000/$3,200–6,400

**▼ Commemorative handkerchief**
An English piece from about 1710 depicting the controversial
academic and politician Dr Sacheverell, with roundels featuring
some of his followers.
£500–1,000/$800–1,600

In the 1830s and 1840s, handkerchiefs reflected contemporary inventions and developments, for example, the Liverpool and Manchester railway in 1831 and the Thames tunnel in 1843, and the various designs for the new Houses of Parliament in the 1840s. Popular heroes were also celebrated such as prize-fighters and rat-catchers. The Great Exhibition of 1851 provided another topic which was represented in a grandiose fashion in the "Exterior View of the Building for the Great Exhibition of 1851", and also in a comic way in "The Greenhorns at the Exhibition ... came up to London for a week to see the Wonders of the World", and "The Great Exhibition 'Wot is to be'".

Moralistic commentary was a favoured subject with titles such as "The Way to Wealth Health & Happiness" and "Fiji before Civilization". In the second half of the 19th century, puzzle handkerchiefs were developed, one notable example being "The Eastern Question 1878", which revealed a portrait of the British Prime Minister Benjamin Disraeli when folded up. Future predictions were also an inspiration. "Womans Rights & What Came of It 1981", from the

1880s, predicted what women would be doing in a hundred years' time while "The Century of Invention Anno Domini 2000", from 1800, looked even further ahead. Racing handkerchiefs were produced too, with an annual one for the Epsom Derby.

Handkerchiefs in a wide variety of subjects can be collected. Some will have a printed date in the title although the piece may actually be later, such as the "Declaration of the Independence of the United States of America July 1776", published in 1840. Some will also have printed names of engravers or publishers in the borders that may indicate the origin of a piece. Occasionally, the name and date of the owner can be found inscribed in ink, generally around the edge.

Whether printed on silk, cotton or linen, they make fascinating documents for recording what was important to contemporary society. The earlier pieces, especially late 18th-century examples, are highly sought after. Handkerchiefs from the late 19th and 20th centuries, although often commemorating interesting events, are generally mass-produced and so less collectable.

**◄ *Tuileries* headscarf**
This headscarf by "Metz" was first printed in 1990, and is a
classic example of the appeal of Hermès scarf illustrations.
The value of recent scarves can be unpredictable.
£50–400/$80–640

**► *Christophe Colombe* headscarf**
This headscarf, depicting Christopher Columbus's
ship at sea, was designed by "De Parcevaux" in 1992
to commemorate the discovery of America.
£50–400/$80–640

# 20th-Century Headscarves

Although scarves and neckerchiefs have both been worn with some style since the early 18th century by fashionable women, the advent of the signed scarf is a 20th-century phenomenon.

Silk squares by the artist and designer Raoul Dufy were some of the first signed scarves. He worked extensively with the famous couturier Paul Poiret in the early years of the 20th century, perfecting various prints and techniques. Poiret was knowledgeable about printing processes, and financed Dufy's workshop for many years. His designs very often feature exquisite prints, sometimes based on his trade mark of a rose, and sometimes based on the historical textiles from his extensive collection. Dufy produced graphically stunning prints in black and white on satin which Poiret used to great effect for fur-trimmed opera coats and cloaks.

Dufy and Poiret parted company when Dufy formed a partnership with the important textile manufacturer, Bianchini-Férier, and he went on to produce numerous designs for them for mass production. His first prints, however, for Poiret had been hand-printed for the luxury market. One of the

most famous is *Le Tennis*, a monochrome print from the 1920s, usually printed in green, of the game being played. As very few of these were actually printed, their value to collectors is high. Any Dufy textile, especially hand-printed, will excite a great deal of interest. If that print can be associated with the couturier Paul Poiret, the value will rise dramatically. Pieces from Poiret's own Atelier Martine are also extremely collectable.

In the 1930s, Elsa Schiaparelli produced some very collectable headscarves with a slightly Surrealist twist. She moved in bohemian circles and included Salvador Dali among her friends, some of her evening dresses using Dali-inspired prints as the fabric. One of the best is illustrated above, in which a silk is printed with *trompe l'oeil* rips to the fabric. She also designed evening headscarves, sometimes in a matching print to the evening ensemble, and sometimes of diaphanous chiffon trimmed with embroidery or appliqué beads. The print may not actually bear her name as Schiaparelli scarves were originally labelled and these labels have often parted company with the scarf. The collector should concentrate on the black and white

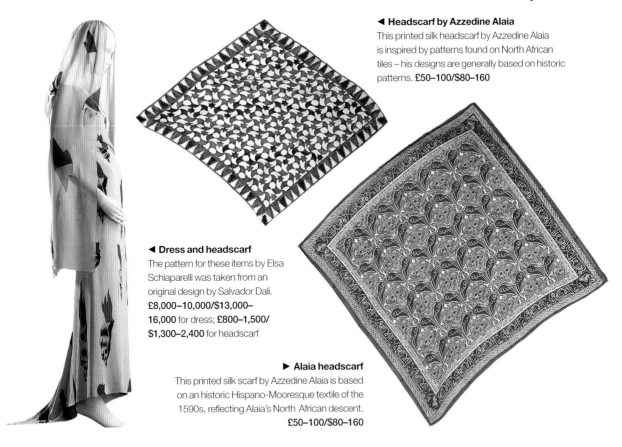

This printed silk headscarf by Azzedine Alaia is inspired by patterns found on North African tiles – his designs are generally based on historic patterns. £50–100/$80–160

◀ **Dress and headscarf**
The pattern for these items by Elsa Schiaparelli was taken from an original design by Salvador Dali. **£8,000–10,000/$13,000–16,000** for dress; **£800–1,500/$1,300–2,400** for headscarf

▶ **Alaia headscarf**
This printed silk scarf by Azzedine Alaia is based on an historic Hispano-Mooresque textile of the 1590s, reflecting Alaia's North African descent. **£50–100/$80–160**

labels of the couture workshop and also be aware of the "shocking pink" silk labels of Schiaparelli designs, which were produced in large numbers under licence in the United States.

The war years saw a proliferation of headscarves of good design as a practical accessory. The English scarf manufacturer Jacqmar produced some witty scarves dotted with clothes coupons and others with contemporary propaganda slogans. These 1940s scarves are a collectable area in themselves, especially if they bear the utility clothing coupon label *CC44*.

The 1950s saw the beginnings of designer marketing. All the major couture houses began to see the potential of accessories. Balenciaga, Givenchy and other rival houses produced printed silk squares for their boutiques. The number of scarves produced each season was never very high, and these are certainly going to be collectable in the future.

Also interesting are the scarves produced by the artist Frederick Ascher. He and his wife commissioned a series of scarf designs from living artists. The roll-call was impressive and included Matisse, Picasso, Patrick Calder, John Piper, and many others. The Maeght Foundation in the South of France also produced a silk scarf every year in very small numbers. At present, the collectable value of these scarves rises and falls with the standing of the individual artist.

In the post-war years, Hermès scarves began to dominate the wider market by their superior quality and successful design. First appearing in 1937, they drew on the visual vocabulary of the leather craftsman, and in particular on the accoutrements of the saddler. Hermès scarves became the choice of the smart woman, including style icons such as Grace Kelly and Jacqueline Onassis. The vocabulary has widened considerably since then. Hermès scarves from before World War II are now very collectable.

In the last twenty years, the Italian house of Versace is the new force in the labelled fashion market for scarves, with its typical multicoloured silk prints. With Gianni Versace's death, these signature prints have become very collectable. However, a number of lesser-known houses have produced interesting pieces. English Eccentrics deserve honourable mention, as does Azzedine Alaia for his fine-quality, original prints based on historical textiles.

▶ **Black-ground cotton**
A printed toile with a black ground from 1850–80, designed for furnishing – the angular fretwork lattice recalls Japonaiserie themes.
£400–600/$640–1,000

▼ **Detail of *toile de Jouy***
A detail of a printed cotton entitled "Les Quatre Saisons" from 1785, with a design made from a copperplate engraving.
£500–600/$800–1,000 per repeat

▲ **Length of *toile de Jouy***
A splendid *toile de Jouy*, printed with flowers and foliage in an Indian style, from the late 18th century.
£400–500/$640–800 per repeat

# Toiles de Jouy

The original and most successful manufacturer of the distinctive printed fabrics from Jouy was Christophe Philippe Oberkampf (1738–1815). He was born in Wurtemberg, Germany, but his family moved to Basel in Switzerland, at that time a centre of the textile-printing industry.

Oberkampf served his apprenticeship as an engraver with some leading manufacturers, including a period in Mulhouse, where print works had been established in 1746 by Jean Jacques Schmaltzer, Samuel Koechlin and Jean Henri Dollfuss. These printworks had expanded to five large manufacturers in 1758 and over a hundred factories in 1759, fuelling the almost insatiable desire of the French public for exotic fabrics. The Revolution decreased demand, and eventually most of the production from Mulhouse was exported to the United States, Mexico and South America, as well as to Egypt, Turkey and Persia.

Oberkampf himself moved to Paris in 1758, where he continued to print cottons in defiance of the embargo on importing foreign goods. He was noticed by a financier at Versailles, who had been forewarned of the imminent lifting of the ban on printing cottons, and hoped to be ahead of the competition when the ban was lifted. With the financier's backing, Oberkampf moved his whole enterprise to the village of Jouy-en-Josas, near the royal palace of Versailles. He installed his brother, Frédéric, as chief engraver. The first chintz was produced in 1760, engraved, printed and dyed by Oberkampf personally. His backing failed soon after, but he called in Swiss money and expertise, and formed a new company, Sarrazin, Demaraise, Oberkampf et Cie.

Oberkampf had chosen his factory site well. Situated near Versailles, aristocratic ladies on their way to court often spotted interesting pieces spread out in the sun to fix the colours. Royal visits followed, and in due course the official title of *Manufacture Royale*. From 1775 to 1780 several grand projects were undertaken for Louis XVI, and Jouy flourished.

▲ **Detail of a *toile de Jouy***
A detail of a dark-ground toile of 1790–1800 – such bold,
colourful images of flowers shining through dark grounds were
the result of the technical brilliance of precision printing at Jouy.
**£400–500/$640–800** per repeat

Procedures were very much the same as printed
cottons produced in Alsace at Mulhouse, but Jouy soon
became known for innovations such as the use of small
intense dots of colour to enrich a tone, known as
*picotage*. In 1770 copper plates were introduced, using
the same principles as for printing etchings. This
allowed for a large repeat with intricate details,
although admittedly only in one colour.

As elsewhere, the factory's main production was in
dress lengths. For this purpose, it brought in fine
muslins and cottons from India or Switzerland, and
printed mainly what were known as *mignatures*, or
small patterned sprigged dress lengths. The year 1772
featured sprigs on white ground in the Indian style, in
the 1780s snuff or dark grounds were introduced, and
in 1805 roller printing was adopted. In 1797 a second
era of prosperity had begun under the Consulate and
Empire, including a visit by the Emperor Napoleon in
1806. Oberkampf himself died in 1815, although the
factory continued in production until 1843.

# Dating *Toiles de Jouy*

▲ **"Les Travaux de la Manufacture de Jouy"**
A charming depiction of the various manufacturing
processes at Jouy by Jean-Baptiste Huet, 1783.
**£500–600/$800–1,000** per repeat

Identifying the date of a *toile de Jouy* can be
difficult, as traditional patterns have often
been revived. Prices differ markedly between an
original 18th-century toile and a 20th-century
copy. Collectors have to analyse more than the
printed pattern to ascertain the date of a toile.

Points to note are first of all the width of the
fabric. Originally, width was limited to the
length a weaver can throw a shuttle, which is
usually about 58cm (23in). However, double
widths are possible, if rare; 19th-century cottons
could be much wider, as they were produced on
mechanical power looms.

The second point is the colour: 18th-century
toiles are predominantly monochrome red, with
the occasional and rare blue toile. Sepia and
mauve dyes became popular in the early 19th
century. Also important is the configuration of
the design. A handblock printed design will be
based on repeats of squares, and if you look
carefully, you will be able to see where each block
begins. Copper rollers are not limited to this
repeat, and can therefore be much bigger and
stretch from edge to edge. Lastly, there is the feel
of the textile in the hand; 20th-century versions
have a very stiff glaze and a loose weave. With
time and experience, a collector will be able to
gauge this without being able to say exactly why
a textile feels 20th century.

**▲ Panel of *toile de Nantes***
The outlines of the printing block are visible on this toile entitled "Achille reconnu par Ulysse" by Favre, Petitpierre et Cie, *c.*1810. **£300–400/$480–640** per repeat

**▼ Panel of *toile de Nantes***
Illustrating the taste for exotic scenes typical of *toiles de Nantes*, this panel entitled "Robinson Crusoé" was printed by Favre, Petitpierre et Cie in *c.*1815. **£300–400/$480–640** per repeat

# *Toiles de Nantes*

*Toiles de Nantes* have generally been considered as the poorer relation to *toiles de Jouy*, lacking the royal patronage which helped encourage new designs and techniques. Production of chintzes at Nantes in Brittany began as a direct result of the lifting of the ban on the production of *Indiennes* (printed cottons) in 1759. Although now land-locked, in the 18th century Nantes was well situated, being a port on the mouth of the Loire, and having strong trading links with the East through the Compagnie des Indes. It also had strong links with Switzerland and therefore had access to both financial backing and the chemical industry which produced the dyes they required.

Nantes has some parallels with Liverpool, as cotton printers in both towns were deeply involved in the slave trade. The trade accounted for 20 per cent of the Nantes' turnover and underpinned much more. It is startling to know that the town sent as many ships to the slave-trading coast of Guinea as all the other maritime ports of France combined. Printed cottons, rifles, gunpowder, spirits and glass would be shipped to Africa to be traded for slaves, who were shipped to the new colonies in French America and the Caribbean. The ships would return from these colonies laden with coffee, sugar, cotton and indigo.

The cottons sent out to Africa were specific to the African market. The entire production was therefore despatched, leaving none to be sold in Europe – no original printed example survives in Nantes of these cottons. However, some of the patterns have been re-discovered in the form of the original copper rollers, many of which are held by the Musée de l'Impression sur Etoffes, Mulhouse.

The main production in Nantes was, as at Jouy, for dress fabrics, that is to say small-scale sprig patterns. Although produced in great quantities, fewer examples have survived than those of the monochrome furnishing prints, which were always a smaller market. These larger copperplate engraved furnishing toiles were luxury items, as their costs included the price of the designer, engraver, the copper and the machinery to print the large repeats. The

▼ **Panel of *toile de Nantes***
This early design entitled "Scènes maritimes, Neptune ou l'empire de la mer" was printed in c.1795 by Maison Petitpierre et Cie in monochrome red. **£400-500/$640-800** per repeat

◄ **Large-scale *toile de Nantes***
This chintz printed by Dubey et Comp., in c.1815, was clearly inspired by Indian flowering tree prints.
**£200–400/$320–640** per repeat

furnishing toiles, also, were carefully stored and survived intact, whereas the cheaper dress cottons were treated more roughly and often recycled.

The first factory was set up by Louis Langevin, a merchant, in 1758 and lasted until 1771. Twenty-five years later, there were nine more factories and 1,200 people employed in printing cottons. Some factories stamped their goods but most did not. Identification of Nantes toiles is therefore not easy. However, it is known that the 18th-century fabrics were mainly red on white ground, with only one blue example being recorded. They were printed with copper inlaid blocks or woodblocks, and some were polychrome. Compared to Jouy toiles, those of Nantes were a little more naïve and less technically accomplished, with designs that are often linked by bridges or waterfalls. Antique ruins, round temples, and a distinctive pine set at an angle on a rocky promontory, together with a taste for exotic scenes, particularly depictions of inhabitants from Asia, Africa and America, were particularly popular themes.

The late 1770s were a period of rapid expansion which saw the beginnings of the most important printers: Maison Petitpierre (1770), Maison Davies (1772) and Maison Pelloutier (1772). The blockade of English goods caused by the American War of Independence, which precluded the import of chintzes from India, was a further spur to production.

In the 19th century, the number of designs based on known prints or lithographs and on popular operas increased, as did designs based on classical mythology. Violet and fawn appeared as colours and polychrome prints disappeared. As a general rule, the white ground of the cotton became filled with pattern and the width of the cotton increased. The quality of the printing also tended to decline.

From producing expensive chintzes with exotic themes for French markets in the 18th century, Nantes in the 19th century was producing a cheap French product for export to the colonies. The collector can still acquire *toiles de Nantes* for reasonable prices, and they are worth taking some time to study and collect.

# Lace & Whitework

## From the 16th to the 19th century: exquisite embellishments for linen, court robes or christening gowns

The study of lace appeals to several different types of collector. On the one hand, laces can be seen as frills and flounces and on the other as a mathematical puzzle. The collector needs to have a good understanding of basic techniques in order to be able to tell Brussels lace from Milanese and to appreciate the technical brilliance of a good piece.

The word "lace" is derived from the Latin *laqueus* meaning "noose", that is a hole outlined by a rope, string or thread. The term therefore covers a great variety of ornamental openwork fabrics formed by the looping, plaiting, twisting or knotting of the threads of flax, silk or other substances, whether by hand or machine.

Broadly speaking, there are two main types of lace – needle lace and bobbin lace. They developed out of the two crafts of needlework and braiding. In the past, needle laces have always been the shared province of both amateur and professional, whereas bobbin laces have traditionally been the domain of the professional lacemaker, with a few notable

exceptions. Today, however, the British Lace Guild has over 8,000 amateur members, most of whom are lacemakers.

Both types of lace began in Italy in the late 16th century. Needle lace makes its first appearance as a decorative insertion between seams of linen chemises. It was often white, but could be made of coloured silks, particularly red. From this humble beginning, needle lace developed into an international commerce of such importance that emperors and kings were forced to pass decrees limiting its import.

In 18th-century England, smuggling of needle lace from Europe was rife. Lace was hidden in loaves, turbans, books, umbrellas and even coffins. Much foreign lace was confiscated by customs officials and burnt, and much has also been lost by burial, since corpses were decked out in their smartest clothes.

In the 16th and 17th centuries, lace was always made from linen, metal or silk thread. Production of the fine linen thread was limited to damp, temperate climates, such as Ireland and Flanders, as the thread was prone to dry out

▲ **Needle lace border**
A border of scalloped needle lace made in Italy early in the 17th century.
£500–600/$800–1,000

◀ **Handkerchief**
Made in Italy in the 1620s, and edged in *punto in aria* (literally "stitches in air"). Always check that the centres have not been replaced.
£500–1,000/
$800–1,600

◀ **Fine linen handkerchief**
An Italian linen handkerchief of the late 16th century with embroidered borders and a cutwork centre.
£1,000–1,500/$1,600–2,400

and break when spun in warmer climates. The centres of production of linen are also, broadly speaking, the lace-producing areas.

Cutwork, in which holes were cut in material and then embroidered, was one of the earliest developments away from the seam insertions of the late 16th century. Small-scale cutwork was fashionable in the 17th century, when it was used extensively on collars, cuffs and even gloves. Portraits of the time go to some length to portray these accurately.

Bobbin lace is produced not with a needle, but by plaiting threads on a pillow. The individual threads are weighted with bobbins, or elongated bone or wood weights, to stop the threads from tangling. This lace developed not from needlework insertions, but from the braiding industry. It is by definition free-standing and not part of the linen it decorates.

The earliest bobbin laces are very simple edgings less than 2.5cm (one inch) deep, used to trim linen. As time progressed, the number of threads increased, allowing ever more complex patterns. The Flemish were the masters of the

art of bobbin lace, with some laces requiring hundreds of bobbins to produce. Certain decorative devices were introduced, such as the wheatear, a decorative bunching of threads to form a tear-shaped raised motif. In France these were known as *point d'esprit*. The plaited links between motifs are known by the French term *brides* (bars or bridges). The dense centres of motifs, which look like linen, are known as clothwork or *toilé*, the glory of Flemish laces.

At first, looking at lace close up is bewildering. However, telling bobbin lace from needle lace is generally not difficult but does require a magnifying glass. The key is to analyse with a cool head. Close up, you will be able to see that a needle lace is made up of buttonhole stitches, whereas bobbin lace looks plaited or woven in the denser areas. One way of checking is to try and follow a single thread. Knowing whether a lace is a bobbin or needle is in one sense unimportant, as you can appreciate its beauty regardless. However, if you are trying to work out when and where a lace was made, it is essential to know how it was made.

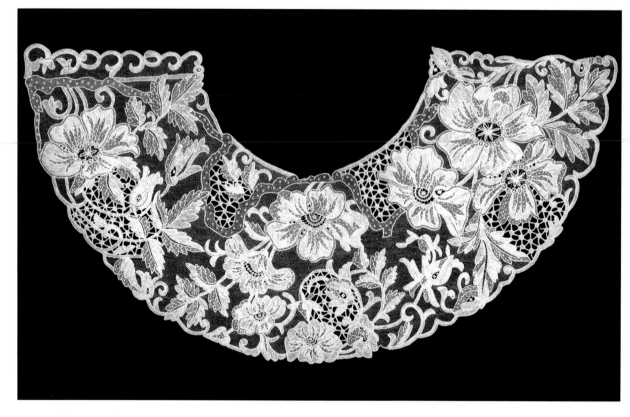

▲ **Burano needle-lace fan leaf**
This fan leaf from Burano, worked in needle lace, dates from the 19th century and is 16cm (6in) deep. **£500–1,000/$800–1,600**

# Italian Needle Laces

Italy is the cradle of lacemaking. It seems that both needle and bobbin laces made their first appearance in Italy – needle lace in the late 16th century and bobbin lace soon afterwards. Italian craftsmen were the best in the world for most of the 17th century. Even in the 20th century, Italy was one of the few countries where the concept of a "bottom drawer" of fine linen for a bride's trousseau was paid more than lip service. Today you will still find an appreciation of fine linen and embroidery, even in the young. A side-effect of this is that many 20th-century linens exist in the style of the 17th century. Care should be taken when dating.

Italian cutwork (*punto tagliato*) in the early 17th century was the finest in Europe and was used to decorate linen, either on tablecloths, or shirts and ruffs. Small-scale cutwork was also used to decorate the starched ruffs of the Italian courtiers. It began as narrow bands of piercing in the early 17th century. As the century progressed and fashions changed, it became mainly associated with trimming linen coverlets and sheets. For reasons of strength the pierced holes had to be based on the linen structure, so that patterns were generally based on squares and were geometric in nature. Patterns were very conservative and continued to be used through the centuries. Today, you may find borders of cutwork detached from their original linen. They are nonetheless collectable. A complete coverlet from the 17th century would be a rare find indeed, whereas a good-quality 19th-century example is not rare and definitely affordable.

Drawn threadwork (*punto tirato*) was one of the glories of 17th-century Italian lace. In the 16th and 17th centuries it is known as *reticella*, when the ground threads of the linen have been removed substantially, leaving a loose grid of threads. These threads were then bound together in geometric patterns, using a needle and fine linen thread. This lace was still used in the 19th century although to less effect, as the 19th-century machine-spun linen threads were much thicker and less supple than 17th-century hand-spun threads.

*Punto in aria* ("stitches in air") is one of the most charming laces of the early 17th century. Based not on

▼ **Needle-lace border**
This delicate border of *punto in aria*
needle lace dates from the 17th century.
£500–1,000/$800–1,600

▲ **Venetian needle-lace panel**
This large 17th-century panel of collectable Venetian *gros point*
needle lace has typical raised and padded crescents.
£3,000–5,000/$4,800–8,000

▲ **Border of *point plat de Venise***
This lace from the 1660s is technically the same as
Venetian *gros point* lace, but lacks the raised crescents.
£200–400/$320–640

the linen ground, but on a foundation of laid threads tacked on to parchment, it was built up from a myriad of tiny buttonhole stitches, and used as a border for lace collars and cuffs. Unlike the laces mentioned above, it was not part of the ground fabric but free-standing, and needed to be sewn on to its linen foundation. It was not based on a grid pattern but on free-flowing flower designs, typically carnations and occasionally daffodils, each worked as a scallop.

By the middle of the 17th century, needle laces were changing to meet a new fashion demand. Plainer silks and velvets became the rage at court, which showed delicate lace off to perfection. The demand for this kind of lace was met by Venetian lacemakers, who produced a lace of bold and exuberant design suited to opulent display. The courts of Spain, Germany and France all adopted it, and although in 1662 Charles II of England issued a proclamation forbidding the selling or importation of "foreign bone-lace", he also granted his lace merchant a licence to continue to import the same for his own family. The annual bills

for laces were enormous. There are several variants of Venetian lace, including *gros point de Venise*, *point plat de Venise*, *point de neige* and *coraline*.

The new collector of Italian needle laces has to know how to avoid two major pitfalls – falling for reassembled 17th-century laces or for 19th-century laces made to 17th-century patterns. The best way to check whether your lace has indeed been "improved", or is in its original form, is to try and follow the pattern with your finger. If you find that a symmetrical flourish suddenly terminates, or changes direction, you may find that the lace has been reassembled. At least half the 17th-century *gros point* laces on the market have been reassembled to some extent. There is a considerable premium on unaltered pieces.

The collector should also beware of the popularity of "Revival" or "Renaissance" laces. In particular, in the 1870s, the lacemakers of Burano, near Venice, created scrupulously accurate copies of early designs. Experience will tell you which is the genuine 17th-century piece and which the 19th-century copy.

▶ **Silver bobbin-lace border**
This silver bobbin-lace border comes from an 18th-century Italian christening blanket.
**£200–250/$320–400** per metre (39½in)

▶ **Silver bobbin-lace border**
This silver bobbin-lace border comes from an 18th-century Italian christening blanket.
**£200–250/$320–400** per metre (39½in)

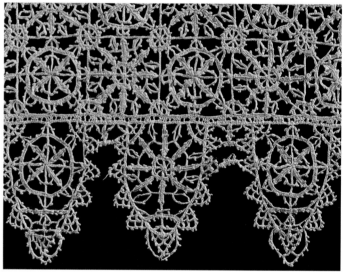

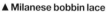

▲ **Milanese bobbin lace**
A flounce of Italian bobbin lace from the hem of a priest's linen alb, with columns of tulips, made in Milan in c.1700.
**£500–1,000/$800–1,600**

# Italian Bobbin Laces

Bobbin laces were first produced in Italy in the late 16th and early 17th centuries, slightly after the appearance of needle laces. They are closely related to the braids and metal laces for which Italy was rightly famous. Most surviving pieces from this early date are small-scale edgings designed to be sewn on to costume and linen. However, needle lace was far more popular than bobbin lace throughout the 17th century. Bobbin lace took over at the beginning of the 18th century, and was produced in many centres, wherever there was a sufficient population to support a lacemaking industry.

In the 17th century Genoa was an important lace-producing city whose reputation was for heavy silk, linen or metal laces used for trimming costumes. The general appearance is of a smooth and solid lace, worked in a series of soft scallops on a narrow header. Laces usually have characteristic wheatears and occasionally plaited loops between each scallop. Popular for most of the 17th century, Genoese laces

can be seen on the costume in portraits of the time, indicating that it was a lace for the special occasion rather than everyday use. The decline in popularity of this lace is probably linked to the changed fashion for cravats rather than flat collars.

Milanese lace was probably the most important of the Italian bobbin laces. It was made from the 17th century and throughout the 18th century, being revived later in the 19th century. It is a part lace, which means that motifs were made separately and then assembled, in the 17th century by using *brides*, or linking threads, and with a round mesh from the mid-18th century. You can see this by looking at the reverse of the bobbin lace, where *brides* will be linked underneath the *toilé*, going from one area of mesh to the next. By the mid-18th century the mesh was widespread. It is a fairly heavy lace and not as fine as its Flemish counterpart. Clothwork loops were particularly popular in the 17th century. The pattern was formed by bobbin-woven tapes, partly folded

◄ **Genoese bobbin-
lace border**
This border of Genoese
bobbin lace of *c.*1600 is
characteristically dense,
with typical wheatear
and tied motifs.
**£100–120/$160–200**
per metre (39½in)

▼ **Bobbin lace border**
This 19th-century Milanese
border is unusual in showing
such a detailed scene of
animals and figures, which
required considerable skill.
**£300–500/$480–800**

◄ **Bobbin lace flounce**
This flounce is from the
early 17th century – note
how the maker has
simulated an edge of the
linen ground along the
side of the scallops.
**£350–450/$560–720**
per metre (39½in)

and sewn to form swirls and flourishes, sometimes woven to shape. These clothwork flourishes were then linked by *brides* into a single piece of lace.

At the beginning of the 17th century, patterns in Milanese lace were formal and baroque, and comparable to the needle laces of Venice. Occasionally, the lace also contained pictorial elements, such as a risen Christ or birds or mermaids. Much of this lace was destined for the Church and is today found in the form of flounces. By the middle of the century the motifs were becoming smaller and spaced more widely, and at the end of the century, the patterns were vermicular and abstract. In Genoa and Milan, as well as Venice and central Europe, tape laces were utilized as a faster method of producing something that resembled *point plat*. The technique used bobbin-made tapes, which could be produced relatively quickly and inexpensively, used in place of clothwork. Tape lace can be identified by the folds in the lace that occur when turning corners. Such laces

can be very fine or rather crude, depending on the thickness of the tape and on the fineness of the filling detail. The pattern is usually embellished by a wide range of decorative fillings which can be bobbin or needle lace, and varies by location. They began in the 17th century and continue to this day in a crude form.

In addition, bobbin lace has always been produced in Italy for the peasant market, usually in bands for trimming costume and made up of thick, durable linen thread after very conservative designs. It can be acquired quite inexpensively, but is notoriously difficult to date given the continuity of patterns from the 16th to the 20th centuries – assigning a date is, in most cases, a matter of instinct.

Italian bobbin laces cover the whole gamut of lace and really can offer something to most collectors. Those setting out to explore the subject may well begin with the inexpensive, dramatic peasant laces of the south of Italy, and work their way towards an exquisite and 17th-century pictorial lace flounce.

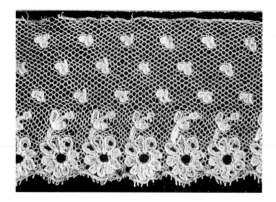

▲ **Detail of Mechlin lace**
An early 19th-century piece – note the thread
*cordonnet* outlining each flower, characteristic of
Mechlin lace. **£20–25/$32–40** per metre (39½in)

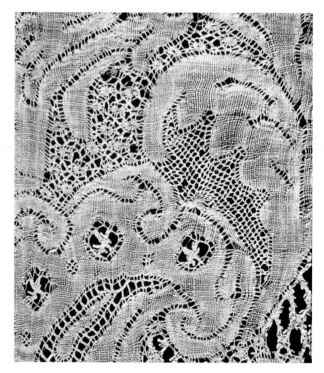

◄ **Valenciennes lappet**
In this technically complex
lace, patterns are outlined by
pinholes rather than threads.
**£400–600/$640–1,000** a pair

▲ **Detail of lappet**
A detail of a Valenciennes
lappet, showing clearly the
characteristic pinholes.
**£400–600/$640–1,000** a pair

# Flemish Laces

Because the spinning and handling of linen thread requires a damp, temperate atmosphere, Flanders was ideally suited to producing the very finest thread on the market. Lacemakers therefore had a unique medium available to them, and were able to produce the finest, most supple of laces.

Even at the beginning of the 17th century, Flemish patterns were more open than Milanese laces and were therefore airier. Spidery, Gothic-pointed scallops gradually became rounder in the manner of Genoese laces of the time. Flemish bobbin laces used a similar design vocabulary to their Italian counterparts, in that the pot of flowers was an ideal motif for a scallop. However, Flemish lace could be supple and have airy clothwork areas where the thicker, less flexible Italian thread could not compete.

In addition, documentary evidence suggests that in the 1630s bobbin lace was cheaper than cutwork. This price advantage did not last long. Soon Flemish lace was as expensive as Italian needle lace – its advantage lay in the quality of the threads and in the business acumen of Flemish merchants, who were in close touch with Paris and able to respond quickly to the demands of fashion. Their success led to Flanders laces and linens being worn by all the crowned heads of Europe until the 18th century.

The different varieties of Flemish laces bear the names of the main lacemaking centres. However, production was spread over several towns in close proximity, and the title is intended to denote a type rather than a place of origin. Binche lace dating from the late 17th and 18th centuries is the favourite of the discerning lace collector. It is a straight lace (one manufactured in a single piece), produced in the form of edging, lace caps and lappets. It is characterized by superb clothwork, with no outlining thread to motifs, of a particular lightness and with a snowflake ground.

Traditionally, Valenciennes lace was very popular for trimming linen undergarments, and a machine version is often used today for silk camisoles. It follows

**◄ Valenciennes lace**
A late 19th-century
border, still with pinholes,
but with a net forming the
main part of the pattern.
**£20–25/$32–40**
per metre (39½in)

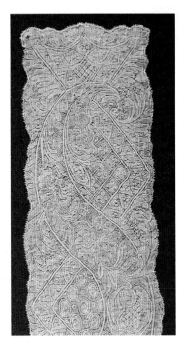

**◄ Valenciennes lappet**
The design of this fine-
quality Valenciennes
lappet from the early
18th century is strongly
influenced by contem-
porary "bizarre" silks.
**£500–1,000/$800–1,600**
for a pair

# Identifying
# Flemish Lace

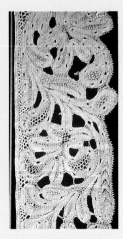

**▲ Milanese lace**
This piece shows the
double *brides* that were
used to link the clothwork
scrolls in Milanese lace,
and dates from the second
half of the 18th century.
**£29–32/$45–52** per
metre (39½in)

**▲ Flemish lace**
This Flemish border dates
from the first half of the 18th
century, and shows each of
the motifs touching the
other, before the need for
single *brides* arose.
**£40–45/$65–72** per
metre (39½in)

In the 17th century, Milanese and Flemish
bobbin laces were quite distinct in terms of
pattern, although they shared the same
technique. Milanese laces of the 17th century
show large areas of clothwork flowers, each
touching the next, while 17th-century Flemish
lace has a more symmetrical and flatter
appearance, with fewer internal patterns.

With the change of fashion from starched
ruff collars to flat collars, the emphasis turned to
a flat, supple lace with patterns that could be seen
at a distance. To achieve this effect, the space
between the patterned clothwork areas of the
laces expanded. The Milanese favoured links of
plaited *brides*; the Flemish began with single *bride*
links but soon developed a mesh ground, against
which the flowers stood out in strong contrast.

Particularly in the early 18th century, it is
difficult to assign a bobbin lace to either Milan or
Flanders. However, checking the type of plaited
*brides* for early 18th-century pieces, and the
ground for later 18th-century laces should give
the collector some clues to work on. With
experience, the feel of the lace in the hand will
also help. Flemish linen is more supple and
slippery than its Milanese counterpart.

its original characteristics of clothwork without an
outlining thread, but with pinholes worked around the
motifs as a decorative element. It was extremely
expensive because of the very fine thread used, and the
vast number of bobbins required by the elaborate
designs. Of less fine quality, Brabant lace is primarily a
furnishing lace, of a cloudy appearance. It is closely
related to English bobbin laces of the West Country.

Mechlin lace is characterized by a single thicker
*cordonnet* (outline). The clothwork motifs are usually
small in scale and worked into a variety of novelty
grounds, including a snowflake ground and *oeil de
perdrix* (partridge eye). It is most plentiful in the early
19th century but of the highest quality in the 1740s. The
18th-century Mechlin laces, particularly cap backs and
lappets, have many admirers. Although reclaimed by
the French, the laces of the Lille area also belong to the
Flemish tradition. They are characteristically cloudy,
with a clear ground, sprigged with small flowers often
with a spotted ground and an outlining *cordonnet*.

▲ **Detail of Brussels lace lappet shown on right**
Worked in a design of a camel ridden by a cherub.
The characteristic tallies of this bobbin lace of the
1690s are well shown in the columns.
**£1,000–1,500/$1,600–2,400** for set

▼ **Brussels lace lappet and matching cap back**
Square-ended lappets are only found in the late 17th and early 18th century.
**£1,000–1,500/$1,600–2,400** for set

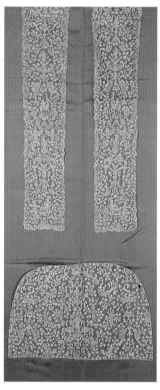

▲ **Pair of bobbin-lace lappets**
Worked with larger flowers characteristic of the mid-18th century,
as are the rounded ends.
**£400–800/$640–1,300** a pair

► **Detail of a lappet**
More net was visible by the 1750s,
with only scattered motifs used.
**£500–800/$800–1,300** a pair

# Brussels Laces

Brussels laces are, geographically and technically, Flemish laces. However, they merit a separate discussion because of their success in reaching virtually all European markets. You may find these laces called *point d'Angleterre*, probably referring to the market destination; this term may also have been a ploy to avoid import restrictions on lace into the United Kingdom. Some lace commentators even take it to refer to laces made in Honiton in the Brussels technique. As the term is confusing it should be treated with caution.

Brussels produced both bobbin and needle laces, although its bobbin laces are the most well known. In the 17th century, its bobbin laces of the finest quality were world-famous, although few pieces from this date have survived. It was worked with a continuous pattern without a mesh ground until the early 18th century, when the characteristic Flemish *réseau* (net) appeared. This *réseau* is hexagonal, with two sides plaited four times and six sides plaited twice.

During the 18th century, Brussels bobbin lace displayed the characteristic veining, where bundles of clothwork are raised, usually as leaf veins, instead of using the single *cordonnet* thread of Mechlin laces to outline motifs. It is seen to great effect on ladies' lappets. Gradually, the cloth motifs became smaller and the mesh more extensive.

Brussels bobbin laces have several variants – the most common is "Brussels mixed lace". This is composed of bobbin lace flowers and leaves, usually linked by *brides*, with small areas of needle lace fillings and flowers. Alternatively, entire veils and shawls were produced of strips of *vrai réseau* or *droschel* sewn together invisibly and then applied with clothwork flowers. This is known as "Brussels appliqué lace". Proper descriptions of this lace should indicate whether the ground is of machine-made or handmade net. A handmade net can double the price of a wedding veil.

*Duchesse* lace is virtually indistinguishable from mixed lace in pattern. However, it does not have

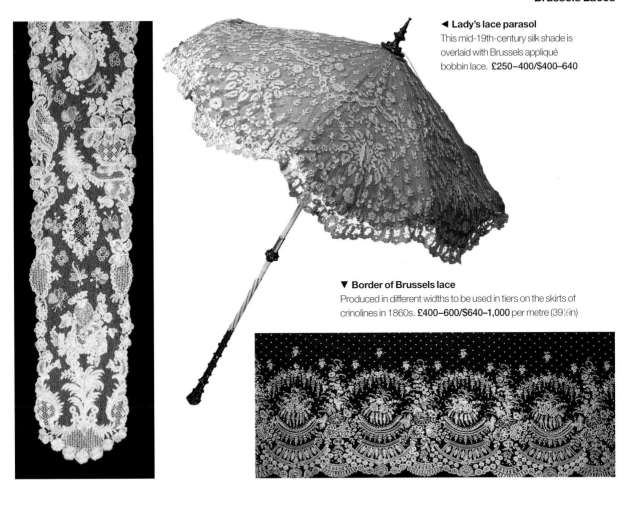

▼ **Border of Brussels lace**
Produced in different widths to be used in tiers on the skirts of crinolines in 1860s. **£400–600/$640–1,000** per metre (39½in)

needle lace inserts but is entirely made of bobbin laces. It is usually a rather heavy lace, which is inexpensive but can be very attractive.

Brussels needle lace from the 18th century is very charming and much sought after by collectors. Usually used on lappets and narrow frills and flounces, it has a dense, button-holed *toilé* and a raised *cordonnet* edge. Fillings are elaborate and diverse.

In the 19th century Brussels needle lace, known as *point de gaze* (literally, gauze stitch), became far more exuberant in design, sharing a design vocabulary with Brussels bobbin lace. However, *point de gaze* is always striving to be three-dimensional. Roses are often worked with raised petals and leaves can be lifted. The more three-dimensional the piece of lace is, the more expensive it will be.

The quality in the 1860s was very high. The best examples can be found in the exhibition catalogues of the day. Top-quality *point de gaze* was exhibited alongside the best industrial products of the day. The firm most associated with exhibition laces of this quality is La Maison Verde-Delisle Frères & Cie, based both in Brussels and Paris. Their most memorable pieces include irises, lilacs and many other naturalistic flowers. When a collector is able to link a lace to a known exhibition, its value will rise considerably.

The most popular items of *point de gaze* are flounces over 4 metres (13ft 2 in) in length which will command four-figure sums. Collars and matching cuffs are also interesting. It is no longer possible to find these pieces in their native Belgium. Cynics might say with some justification that they have all been cut up into individual flowers and leaves and sold in glass medallions to the tourist trade.

The high prices fetched by Brussels laces are not related to the rarity of the lace or indeed the quality but to a particular decorative appeal. With the exception of the very finest pieces, these laces are not bought by the experienced collector, but appeal to a wider, less knowledgeable, but no less enthusiastic audience.

**▲ Detail of *point de France* needle-lace flounce**
This design is possibly by Bérain, one of the most influential court artists employed by Colbert to design laces at Alençon in the 17th century. £5,000–15,000/$8,000–23,000 for 3 by 1m (10 by 3ft)

**▼ Detail of *point de France* lace**
Showing the hexagonal mesh with buttonhole *picots* used to depict a classical figure in military dress. 17th century. £6000–8000/$10,000–13,000 per metre (39½in)

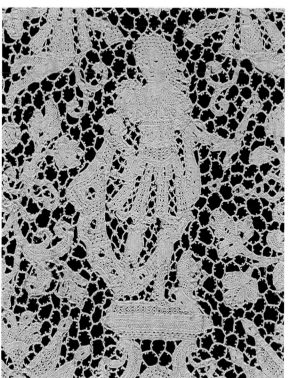

# French Laces

France has always been a major producer of both bobbin and needle laces. In the first half of the 17th century, Italy still dominated both the silk and the lace industry. Huge sums were spent by the court of Louis XIV on formal attire – given that the French have always been passionate about dress, the drain on the exchequer and indeed on the gold reserves of the country was immense, with fortunes heading towards Venice and Genoa for laces, velvets and brocades.

Colbert, chief minister to Louis XIV, imposed draconian sumptuary laws not only forbidding the import of foreign laces and silks, but making French lace and silks compulsory for wear at court. At one stroke, the silk and lace industries of France were presented with a discerning market hungry for novelty and for quality.

In 1665, Colbert set up a lace factory at Alençon in Normandy, encouraging the best court artists, such as Bérain, to design lace patterns. The needle lace that was produced as a result won the approval of the King and was then given the name of *point de France*.

The lace is characterized by formal devices, of a strictly symmetrical disposition, linked by hexagonal mesh with buttonhole-stitched *picots*. There can also be some raised work. It was designed to be viewed flat originally, and was therefore a heavy lace. The name of *point de France* is one to conjure with, being one of the finest laces ever produced, and having been designed by the foremost artists of the day and produced to the highest possible standards. Until the end of the 17th century, there was nothing to match it. Fashions then changed to use the lighter, draped laces and the spotlight moved to other laces. These lighter needle-lace variants were called Alençon, Argentan and Argentella laces. Geographically, they are produced in a very small area of France, and their centres of production may indeed overlap.

Alençon is the most plentiful of these, as its simpler *réseau* made it quicker and cheaper to produce, and is the one that the collector will come across regularly. It is characterized by a *cordonnet* of *picots* stiffened with a horsehair. Usually, the

◀ **Flounce of Alençon lace**
Very finely worked. A close-up would reveal a horsehair around each motif used to loop buttonhole stitches.
**£1,000–2,000/ $1,600–3,200**
for 3 metres (9ft 10in)

▼ **Argentan flounce**
A flounce of French Argentan lace with an extensive *réseau*, made in the late 18th century.
**£500–600/$800–1,000**
per metre (39½in)

horsehair has been pulled out. The ground of this delicate lace is a twisted mesh which is in itself fragile and can often be snagged by the horsehairs. This kind of lace was revived in 1810 by Napoleon for his second wife, Marie Louise of Austria.

French bobbin laces were not as commercially important as its needle laces. However, they were substantial contributors to local economies. Valenciennes laces are usually grouped with the technically similar Flemish laces rather than French laces. Lille is very close to Valenciennes but the laces produced were French in style, inasmuch as the mesh ground were mostly a French *réseau* or net. The designs are usually very simple, with very little cloth work, and the ground is often spotted. There is a thread *cordonnet* around each motif.

Chantilly laces were mostly executed in black silk although white examples are known from the 19th century. The black dye of the 18th century used iron as a mordant. As a result, the silks tended to rot quickly. This may explain why so little black lace from before the late 19th century survives. Certainly 18th-century Chantilly lace is difficult to identify, even though production was in full swing between 1740 and 1785 under royal patronage.

Like most French laces, its production virtually ceased during the Revolution and was revived by Napoleon in 1804, who, in the royal tradition, decreed that only Alençon and Chantilly laces were to be worn at court. Production continued into the 20th century in poorer-quality laces. Chantilly designs of the 19th century are classical, with a preponderance of cherubs, roses and other naturalistically depicted flowers.

Chantilly-type laces were produced in French towns such as Le Puy, Calvados, Caen and Bayeux and machine copies were produced in huge quantities both at the time and in the 20th century. Handmade Chantilly is really the only black lace to realize larger sums on the open market. Machine or handmade copies are available for very small sums. It therefore makes sense to be quite sure of your attribution before buying any black lace.

◀ **Detail of needle-lace border**
This lace border dates from around 1620
– by the 18th century such laces had
become known as Hollie Point.
£400–600/$640–1,000 per metre (39½in)

▲ **Flounce of furnishing lace**
Bobbin lace in the Brussels technique, but made in Devon.
The palmettes have spiral motifs known as "turkey tails",
c.1760. £400–600/$640–1,000 per metre (39½in)

▶ **Collar of Honiton bobbin lace**
The roses on this collar are unmistakably English despite
the Brussels technique. £300–400/$500–640

# English and Irish Laces

England produced bobbin and needle laces from
the 17th century onwards. London was the centre
of the metal lace industry, worth a considerable sum
every year to the City of London.

Bobbin laces were developing along a separate
path in the Midlands and the West Country. It is
thought that Flemish refugees brought with them the
technical knowledge to set up a sophisticated lace
industry. Certainly, the type of lace produced at
Honiton in Devon and Brussels is technically very
close, if not identical at times. The influx of French
Huguenots in the 17th century to the Midlands is said
to be the reason why Bedfordshire laces also have some
French features.

Like its Flemish counterpart, Honiton lace *toilé* is
made separately and then held in place by a variety of
stitches. These can be plaited or needle-made *brides*, or
indeed a twisted mesh ground of net stitch. When the
latter is used, the characteristic Honiton "leadlights"
appear. They are small, rectangular tallies in the net,
usually forming a diaper pattern. The clothwork

patterns usually consist of net butterflies, roses,
typically with crosshatched leadlight centres, and
veined leaves. Brussels has always been ready to claim
good Honiton pieces as Brussels lace and conversely, to
suggest that poor-quality pieces of Brussels lace might
in fact be English!

Following recent research, the tide seems to be
turning in this respect. Many good-quality Flemish
style laces are now regularly described as "Devon
lace". There is now agreement that certain motifs,
such as the spirals known as "turkey tails" and "slugs"
are probably English.

As a result of the classification problems, it might
appear that Honiton laces only began to be produced
in quantity in the 19th century. It is certainly true that
the 19th century produced large quantities of bobbin
lace which is still available, frequently at affordable
prices. Early 19th-century Honiton lace was mainly
applied to handmade net bonnet veils, aprons and
caps. Later in the century machine net was used extensively and the quality of the motifs fell considerably.

**▲ Detail of a silver lace stomacher**
A stomacher fitted into the front of an open robe, linking both sides of the bodice, and was often decoratively laced. This silver bobbin lace is English, from the mid-18th century. **£600–1,000/$1,000–1,600**

**◄ Pair of bobbin lace lappets**
These fine-quality lappets of the 1700s are worked with unusual portrait vignettes. **£1,000–2,000/$1,600–3,200** a pair

Honiton seems to have been a domestic lace rather than a lace for the big occasion, with the notable exception of royal commissions – Mrs Treadwin of Exeter made the veil for Queen Victoria's wedding. Out of an industry apparently content to produce pretty trifles sprang, fully formed, a piece of lace of the highest quality which the Queen continued to wear in various ways throughout her life.

For the purposes of lace classification, the Midlands includes Buckinghamshire, Bedfordshire, Northampton, Wiltshire and Sussex. Bucks Point was the most widespread Midlands lace and shows the widest stitch vocabulary. It is made of cotton, with a thicker, silkier *cordonnet*, and the ground is worked in diagonal lines. Designs are simple flowers. It can be expensive when attributed to a known lacemaker. The main body of collectors appear to be lacemakers who appreciate its technical merits.

Bedfordshire Maltese was produced in direct response to the popularity of Maltese lace. It is, however, only a silk lace in black and a cotton lace in the white version. Prices only rise above the very accessible when pieces can be attributed to Thomas Lester (1838–1909), an enterprising and talented lacemaker. An excellent collection can be found in the Cecil Higgins Museum in Bedfordshire.

A very distinctive English lace is the needle lace known as Hollie Point. This is a small-scale lace that was used on babies' first shirts and cap backs, occasionally even on samplers – this was particularly the case in Pennsylvania. The panels consisted of rows of buttonhole stitches with the pattern picked out by gaps in the rows. Curiously, the same technique was employed in coloured silks by the Chinese in the 14th century, and is then known as needle looping.

Like Burano and Bayeux, Ireland produced "Revival" laces in the style of the 17th century. However, independently, Youghal laces appeared in the 1840s as a response to the potato famine. Nicely designed with bold flowers worked in varying shades, on a loose hexagonal mesh, they can be very fine and have an enthusiastic following.

**◀ Lady's cuff**
White cotton, perhaps from
Carrickmacross in Ireland,
made in the late 19th or
early 20th century.
**£20–40/$32–64**

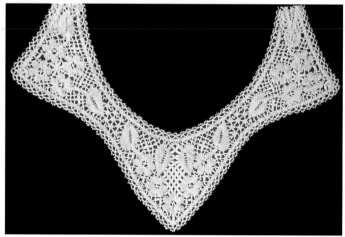

**◀ Linen cover**
A 19th-century piece in the
17th-century style, with
cutwork decoration.
**£500–1,000/$800–1,600**

**▲ Lady's collar**
A lace collar worked in about 1900,
which seems to be the work of an amateur.
Such pieces can be purchased at very
reasonable prices. **£20–40/$32–64**

# Table Linen, Damask and Whitework

The appreciation of linen damask is, as yet, not widespread as the patterns woven into table-cloths are sometimes barely noticeable. However, early linen damasks of the 17th and 18th centuries, are well worth a second look. Patterns combine a flair for graphic design with historical and evangelical propaganda. Collecting these damasks therefore appeals to historians as well as textile enthusiasts.

Damask is a warp-faced textile in which the pattern is picked out by changing the proportion of warp thread visible on the front of the textile. It is usually of one colour, but can be found woven in red and yellow, or blue and white. The reverse of the textile is a negative image of the front – where the front is satin, the back is plain and vice versa. The texture of the linen in the hand is cool and flexible and is often mistaken for silk.

Designs fall into several categories. Biblical scenes from the Old Testament are popular, such as Cain and Abel, various scenes with King David, the Judgement of Solomon and the ever-popular Susannah and the Elders. The second distinct category is commemo-rative of famous battle scenes and conquests by various European monarchs. The main centres of production were Holland, Germany (particularly in Saxony and Silesia), Sweden, Scotland (where Edinburgh and Dunfermline were the main centres), and Lisburn in Ireland. The customers for damasks were international. The collector has to be cautious in dating damasks, as the most popular historical patterns were occasionally repeated in later centuries. Floral patterns are easier to date as they can usually be compared with contemporary silk patterns.

Because of the strength of the fibre, a substantial number of linen tablecloths and napkins have survived. In the 17th and 18th centuries, cloths are usually around 2 metres (6½ft) square, and the napkins just under 1 metre (3¼ft) square. The latter are often mistaken for small tablecloths, and adopted more familiar sizes only in the 19th century.

Dining habits in the mid-19th century changed towards the more formal table. Large damask banqueting cloths appeared along with small napkins. Complete sets of banqueting cloths and matching

▲ **Lace insertion**
Detail of a shoulder insertion on a 17th-century shirt showing needlework links of the kind which developed into needle lace.
£500–1,000/$800–1,600 for a shirt of this date

▲ **Linen coif or cap**
This 17th-century English coif is embroidered in white with cutwork details.
£2,000–4,000/
$3,200–6,400

◄ **Whitework sampler**
A rare 18th-century sampler where each grid is worked with a different whitework pattern.
£1,000–1,500/
$1,600–2,400

napkins are sought after both by linen collectors and by those seeking to cover antique furniture.

It was only in the second half of the 19th century that furnishing fashions included covers in linen and lace. Pictures of 1860s interiors show decorative cloths on tables and chairs, allegedly because Victorians became embarrassed at the sight of a table leg "undressed". In any case, it is certainly true that white cloths would lighten a room full of the heavy and dark furniture of the period.

By the end of the century, decorative mats, teacloths, napkins and dressing-table sets were standard in every middle-class house. Large numbers of them have survived and are now largely unloved by the general public. The skills and indeed the servants to launder these items belong to a bygone era, and they can be acquired at comparatively little expense. The situation is different in countries such as Italy and Spain, where such linens are still very popular.

Cutwork is really a precursor of 16th-century needle lace. Examples from the 16th and 17th centuries are very expensive and rare. However, 19th- and early 20th-century cutwork is affordable and attractive. One of the most popular types to collectors is Richelieu work. This is not only produced in France but also today in China. A large cotton cloth is pierced with arabesques, cupids or flowers. Each edge is then oversewn to stop fraying. This was generally done in white in the 19th century and in ecru (the greyish colour of unwashed linen) in the 20th century. Extraordinarily elaborate tablecloths and matching napkins are still available at reasonable sums compared to new table linen from ordinary department stores.

Marcella coverlets are another popular collectors' item, "marcella" being a corruption of "Marseilles", for centuries famous for producing quilted coverlets. Marseilles quilters used a thin cord sandwiched between two layers of silk and wadding. Lines of running stitch either side of the cord raise the pattern. Marcella coverlets imitate this effect but are, in fact, woven not handmade. They are extremely hard-wearing. Patterns celebrating Queen Victoria's Diamond Jubilee or other important events are more desirable than simple floral motifs.

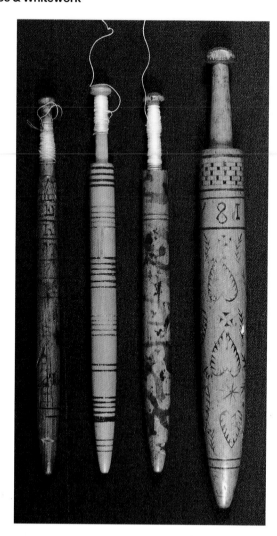

◄ **Wooden bobbins**
A selection of the type used in the West Country in the 19th century, the most elaborate on the right.
**£20–150/$32–$240** each

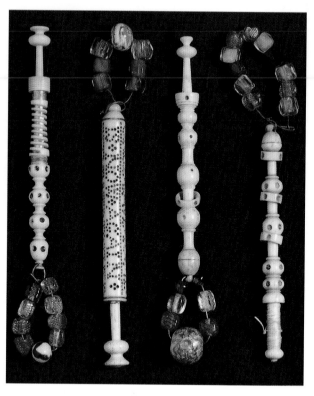

▲ **Bone bobbins**
A selection of the East Midlands type, including two (right) with "gingles" or hoops, and one (second from left) with inscription. **£50–100/$80–160** each

# Lace Bobbins and Ayrshire Needlework

Bobbin lace is essentially plaited thread. In order to keep the many threads in order and to stop them tangling, each thread is wrapped around a turned bobbin and kept hanging straight by its weight.

Bobbins can be serviceable or elaborate. In theory, a simple lead stick would be sufficient to keep the threads stable. In practice, the lacemakers used carved, painted, beaded and turned bobbins. In a practical way, easily differentiated bobbins were also easier to follow through the pattern. Materials were mainly wood and bone, either in natural ivory or stained red or green. "Tiger" bobbins were set with metal bands in chevrons, "leopard" bobbins spotted with nail heads.

A further level of interest was added by the fact that it became a tradition for a boy to carve and inscribe a bobbin for his sweetheart. Some messages are cryptic and only made sense to the sweetheart,

others are in code, and the most elaborate are carved on a spiral around the bobbin. The message can only be read if you slowly turn the bobbin in your hand.

Each region has its own peculiarities, depending on its lacemaking techniques. Honiton bobbins are long, tapering to a point, and often incised and stained in red and black. Early 19th-century bobbins are often carved with anchors and seascapes, and may have been carved by sailors on ships. They are comparatively rare and keenly collected.

The most common are from the East Midlands. They are of bone and wood, with rounded ends. Most are further weighted by a spangle or bead on a copper loop. The largest and most elaborate bead, usually central, is often of Venetian glass. The most collectable are known as "Kitty Fisher spangles", the large beads resembling the said Kitty's eyes.

◄ **Ayrshire christening robe**
A typical Ayrshire christening robe for a girl – robes for girls have the "V" of the bodice tucked into the waistband. The robe's length and high waistline suggest an early 19th-century date. **£300–500/$480–800**

▲ **Ayrshire embroidery**
A detail from the hem of an early 19th-century christening robe. The needlework fillings to the open flower centres are typical.
**£300–500/$480-800** for a whole robe

The county of Ayrshire is located just south of Glasgow on the Firth of Clyde in Scotland. In the 19th century it was a poor and rural area, with life centred on the Church and the family. At births, marriages and deaths the finest linen available was required. Young girls began to prepare for their future roles by embroidering sheets, handkerchiefs, robes and, of course, baby clothes.

A certain Mrs Jamieson, wife of a cotton-merchant in Ayr, seems to have been the mainspring of the organization of this local craft into an industry. Other merchants followed in her path, mainly based in nearby Glasgow, and it is said that in the 1830s, three hundred women were employed in this work.

The characteristic which differentiates Ayrshire needlework from other whitework is the kind of needlework inserts used in the flower centres and around the hems. Ayrshire fillings are some of the finest you will find, particularly on christening robes of fine cotton. As a rule, an early 19th-century robe will be twice the length of a baby, whereas a robe of around 1900 will be just long enough to cover the baby's feet. The bodice has a triangular front, with the point at the waist. It is said that boys' robes have the point showing, and girls' robes have the point tucked into the waistband. There is usually an embroidered ruffle from shoulder to waist.

Ayrshire robes appear on the market only rarely, usually from unexpected dispersals of family possessions. The stories attached to them are often chronologically questionable but of immense significance to the vendor. Family histories usually employ a rather hazy timescale, and the unit to remember is that a generation lasts only about 25 years.

# Quilts

## From the 18th century on: a folk art that records the thrift of both maker and community

Quilting and patchwork are two textile techniques that appear to have been used throughout history. Both are of an extremely practical as well as decorative nature. Quilting, in particular, has been used in clothing to supply both protection and warmth, and is found in Middle Eastern and Far Eastern examples, as well as in Europe.

The bedcoverings that we associate with this terminology can be divided into categories depending on how they have been worked. These are primarily appliqué, piecing and all-over quilting. Some bedcovers, and particularly earlier examples, can be a combination of various techniques. It can be difficult to generalize about the origin of various techniques and patterns because of the extent of cross-pollination of ideas between communities. Britain held sway in the late 18th and early 19th centuries, and ideas were taken to America by early colonists. Here, an independent tradition developed, although

again the interaction between communities and the westward expansion of the country means it can be difficult to generalize about the regional origins of patterns.

The history of quilting and patchwork is also tied closely to the mechanization of the textile industry, particularly developments in printing cotton during the late 18th and early 19th centuries. Some of the earliest coverlets to survive are appliqué. This stemmed from the fashion for Indian chintz that was imported into Europe from the 17th century, becoming so popular that its import was banned in 1701.

This meant that any chintz was highly prized, and when worn out, covers would be cut up and put to another use, leading to the development of *broderie perse* (French for Persian embroidery). Essentially, chintz cut-outs are applied to a cotton or linen ground, usually white. These often include exotic birds such as pheasants, and sometimes a tree of life as a central feature, following the Indian manner. Sometimes, borders are pieced from patches of

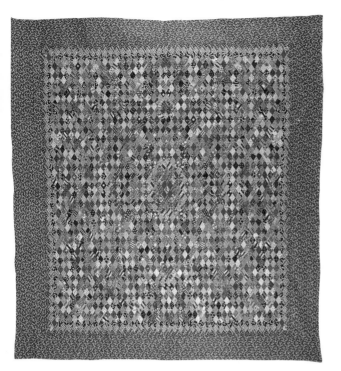

◀ **Patchwork quilt**
A patchwork quilt of tiny diamond-shaped
pieces, from the mid-19th century.
£400–800/$640–1,300

◀ **Quilted silk robe**
An open robe of pale blue silk of the 1730s, quilted with diamond
diaper. Both attractive and practical, this warm garment was an
"undress" robe for informal occasions.
£3,000–5,000/$4,800–8,000

▼ *Broderie perse* **quilt**
The appliquéd chintz design depicts a tree with
birds – the chintz is 18th century, the quilt early
19th century. £1,000–1,500/$1,600–2,400

chintz, but they are rarely quilted. This type
of coverlet represents workmanship from the
wealthy and affluent households that could
afford to buy the imported or printed pieces.
These coverlets are generally English, but they
also seem to have been popular in the southern
states of America.

Wholecloth quilts are also commonly found.
The emphasis here is on the quilting rather than
forming a pattern from various fabrics, whether
through piecing or appliqué. It tends to be more
of a British tradition although wholecloth quilts
are found in America.

Welsh wholecloth quilts tend to maintain
an 18th-century style: a central medallion
surrounded by borders. Strip quilts are also
found in Wales and the north of England. An
odd number of stripes were put together, either
quilted within each strip or as a whole. As in
America, it can be difficult to specify the
regional origin of a quilt, especially as there do
not seem to have been any conscious regional
patterns until the 20th century. Also, there was

some interchange of ideas with America, with
the continuing emigration of relatives to the
new world.

Generally, quilting patterns such as spirals
and veined leaves have come to be associated
with Welsh quilts, and feather motifs and roses
with quilts from the north of England, that is
primarily the counties of Durham and
Northumberland. Hearts are associated, not
surprisingly, with quilts made to celebrate a
marriage. Strip quilts, particularly in turkey red
dye with white, were also popular in the north of
England. In the late 19th century, printed
cottons were used to make wholecloth quilts,
often printed with Paisley-style or Art Nouveau
patterns. In the early 20th century, cotton sateen
was a popular choice of fabric. This has a slight
sheen to the surface and is often found in pastel
shades reflecting the fashions of the time. While
*broderie perse* coverlets remain highly sought
after in today's open market, 19th- and 20th-
century wholecloth quilts can still be found at
very reasonable prices.

**▲ "Tumbling Block" quilt**
The cotton is taken from dresses of the 1790s
to the 1830s, made up into a patchwork quilt in
the 1840s. The materials would suggest that
this is probably English in origin.
£600–1,000/$1,000–1,600

**▼ Quilt with a bullfight**
Probably Spanish, this mid-19th-century quilt
is printed with a bullfight and appliquéd with a
central coronet and crest.
£200–400/$320–640

# Piecing and Patchwork

The British cotton industry was established in the late 18th century, and by the early 19th century supplied a large amount of decorative printed cottons to America, the quantity at first stifling local industry. As printed-cotton production increased, it was no longer an expensive luxury, and cheap fabrics were produced for dresses as well as furnishings. It is scraps from these that were often used as shaped patches, pieced together to form coverlets.

Early 19th-century patchwork coverlets often show the same form as 18th-century English quilting: a central medallion within various frames and borders. In the 1820s and 1830s, many varieties of chintz were used, depending on availability, to form different patterns. Geometric-shaped patches were usual so as not to waste any fabric. After 1840, the vogue for chintz waned, and as fabric became even cheaper, quiltmakers bought lengths specifically to make coverlets, restricting the number and types of material used so that the colour could emphasize a particular pattern. For example, pink and brown, and other brash, lurid combinations were popular in the 1840s, while red and green on a white ground was common from the mid-19th century until the late 19th century. These fabrics were not all necessarily printed, some being plain. White cotton was the cheapest fabric available and the red was achieved by using turkey red dye, developed in the early 19th century.

From the 1830s, with the development of roller printing, mass-produced printed cottons became widely available, meaning a greater range of colours and designs at a cheaper price. By the mid-19th century, "cheater cloth" was produced, a roller-printed cotton that looked like a patchwork top without the

**▲ "Log Cabin" quilt**
Both the cottons and the silks used in this patchwork quilt date from the mid-19th century. This pattern became very popular after the American Civil War of 1861–5.
£400–800/$640–1,300

**▼ Patchwork "album" quilt**
Made of individual patchwork and appliqué squares, such pieces were sometimes embroidered by friends and family to be assembled as an album. These cottons date from the early 19th century.
£400–800/$640–1,300

necessity of any work. It is also in this period that the original patterns for geometric quilt blocks were published in America, in 1835.

Square blocks were worked one at a time, which could then be sewn together to complete the coverlet. This was a less cumbersome method than using a quilt frame to work a wholecloth piece and was more suited to colonial life. The block patterns could either be worked through piecing or appliqué, or a combination of both. They were often finished with quilting too, usually outlining the pattern with various infill patterns, such as crosshatching or waves, on the unworked ground.

Although women predominantly carried out quilting and patchwork, some men also made coverlets. These tended to be either tailors using up surplus fabric or men in the armed forces. Examples of "uniform" patchwork survive, pieced from wool, perhaps taken from uniforms, often said to be those of the Crimean War. However, without specific documentation, these pieces can be difficult to identify.

British patchwork coverlets in the 19th century tend to be based more on "mosaic"patterns: single geometric shapes put together to form patterns such as "Tumbling Block". However the influence of American block patterns was increasingly felt, and it becomes very difficult to determine the origin of a coverlet without knowledge of the maker. Piecing and quilting enjoyed a revival in the 1920s and 1930s in both countries. New patterns were developed such as "Sun Bonnet Sun" and "Ice Cream Cones". Coverlets from this era can sometimes be identified by their colouring, which tends to be pastel shades, often incorporating the floral prints that can also be seen in the dress materials of the 1930s.

**▲ Amish patchwork quilt**
Although the Amish do not use representational motifs, this
pattern is known as "Churn Dash" or "Monkey Wrench", late
19th century. **£700–1,000/$1,200–1,600**

**▼ Amish patchwork quilt**
In typical mid-West colours, and made in Milton, Iowa, *c.*1929.
**£800–1,000/$1,300–1,600**

# American Quilts

In the mid-19th century, there was a fashion for album or friendship quilts in America. Squares were worked by different people, either family members or friends, and then joined together to form the whole piece. It has been speculated that this was due to the westward expansion of the country, and these quilts provided a memento of a previous life for western settlers. The most elaborate examples of this type were worked in Baltimore, Maryland, between 1843 and 1853. As Baltimore was a busy port, there was easy access to incoming fabrics from Britain and France. Likewise autograph quilts can be found, signed and then embroidered, to commemorate a particular event in America or Britain. Coverlets worked with names and dates, and sometimes location, are much sought after by collectors.

The Civil War had a major effect on quiltmaking in America. As well as inspiring work incorporating patriotic symbols such as flags and eagles, it also led to the more general use of the sewing-machine. Developed in the 1850s, its first widespread use was for sewing uniforms. After the war, it was soon used to piece patchwork tops. The popular "Log Cabin" pattern, with its many variations, also seems to have developed after the Civil War in America, although there is some debate as to whether the actual origin of this pattern is American or British .

Names developed for the many different block patterns used, taken from various sources including the Bible, historical events and the landscape, giving rise to titles such as "Bear Paws", "Turkey Tracks" and "Wild Goose Chase". Some patterns were symbolic, for example oak leaves equalling long life, and pineapples suggesting hospitality. However, many different names for the same pattern appear, dependent on the region in which it was woven, and even the particular family tradition. Quilts were exhibited at agricultural and manufacturing fairs, giving an opportunity for their makers to exchange ideas and patterns. It was not until the 1890s that names for patterns were first standardized and printed patterns had widespread usage.

**▶ Patchwork pocket**
The cotton patches are a mixture of late 18th and early 19th-century fabrics.
£400–600/$640–1,000

**▼ Jacquard cover**
Woven with the signature of the maker, Benjamin Lichty of Bristol, Ohio, 1848.
£400–600/$640–1,000

**◀ Jacquard coverlet**
Signed *L A Wright, 1836*, the individual who commissioned the quilt. A lion in the corner tells us that it was woven by Harry Tyler. £300–600/$500–1,000

Quilts made by the Amish communities are a distinct group of work that is highly sought after. Descended from European Anabaptists, their quilt-making is governed by their religious beliefs. Any design is non-representational and the piecing of fabric with patterns is forbidden. The use of small pieces is also considered worldly, so bold, simple geometric designs are generally used. These are usually in unusual colour combinations, often in brilliant hues, although they generally never include white, against a dark ground. The two major settlements of the Amish community are in the eastern United States and the Midwest. Both make quilts although there are some differences in design. The pieces from the eastern states tend to be worked around the idea of a central medallion, while those in the Midwest repeat all-over blocks, perhaps influenced more by the traditional designs of their non-Amish neighbours. Quilting must always be by hand, although elaborate patterns are allowed and are sometimes worked in a contrasting colour thread.

There are no known Amish quilts dated before 1849, which suggests they learnt quilting techniques from their neighbours, probably colonial settlers from Britain. This again emphasizes the cross-fertilization of ideas in quilting and piecing that occurred throughout the 19th century. However Amish quilts can be difficult to date without knowledge of their history, as they do not use patterned fabric, always one of the best ways to establish dating for pieced coverlets.

In contrast to patchwork and quilting, Jacquard-weave coverlets were developed in America by professional itinerant weavers, usually men, from the late 1820s onwards, when the Jacquard attachment was introduced from France. These coverlets are woven in at least two colours of cotton or linen and wool, in a double weave, so that they are reversible. Where more than two colours are used, a rainbow or striped effect sometimes develops. Motifs include flowers, animals and patriotic symbols, and they often incorporate a date and a name, either of the person for whom the coverlet was made, or of the weaver himself.

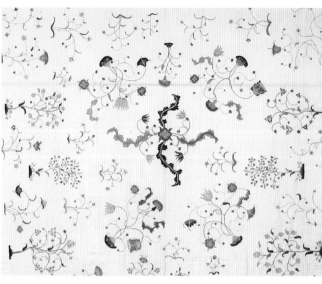

◀ **Pair of crewelwork curtains**
The slate blue and pinks of these curtains are typical of the 19th-century versions of English crewelwork. **£1,000–1,500/$1,600–2,400**

▲ **Crewelwork coverlet**
Embroidered in coloured wools with spindly flower sprays typical of American crewelwork, 18th century. **£3,000–5,000/$4,800–8,000**

# Coverlets

Whitework coverlets were generally popular from the 18th century onwards. Much original 18th-century quilting was worked with cording and stuffing entirely in white, the raised-work detailing emphasizing the design. Patterns were usually floral, reflecting contemporary embroidery and silk patterns, although chinoiserie and Indian-style motifs were not uncommon. Similar coverlets can be found worked in yellow silk threads, also a chinoiserie influence as yellow was associated with China in the European mind, being the Imperial colour.

In America, whitework coverlets were at their most popular between 1790 and 1840. Perhaps mirroring this, candlewick coverlets also found favour in this period – all white, worked against a cotton or linen ground, the design was picked out in relief by embroidering with candlewicking, a coarse cotton thread, often in loops or tufts. Some early 19th-century examples can be found with dates and initials.

As weaving technology progressed throughout the 19th century, designs for white woven cotton coverlets became more elaborate as their price decreased due to mass production. These could have fairly simple patterns for everyday usage or be woven to commemorate a particular event such as a jubilee of Queen

Victoria. These more complex examples may have a factory name woven in around the edge. Marcella coverlets were also popular in the second half of the 19th century (*see* p.137).

It is sometimes possible to find printed cotton coverlets and bed hangings, usually pieced from various-sized panels of the same print, some of which are also quilted. The most desirable are those pieced from known prints produced by manufacturers such as Jouy. Others represent good documents of the age in which they were produced, ones from the 1860s, for example, often being striped and with large-scale naturalistic flowers.

Crewelwork coverlets, along with attendant bed curtains, have a long history and are perennially popular, commanding high prices on the open market. The name comes from the crewel, or large-eyed needle, which used a thick worsted wool thread with a slight sheen and a loose twist. The embroidery can be worked in various stitches, including long and short stitches, couching, stem and buttonhole. It first became popular in the 17th century, the style of pattern closely following developments in other textiles such as silk design. However, crewelwork soon picked up outside influences from India and China, and by the

◄ **French crewelwork wall-hanging**
Probably made for a four-poster bed, in 18th-century style, but worked in the 19th century. **£500–800/$800–1,300**

▲ **Detail of crewelwork bedhanging**
An early 18th-century piece, with a Chinese-inspired central phoenix.
**£5000–6000/$8000–9600**

▲ **Detail of crewelwork hanging**
Both the colouring and the design of this attractive hanging are typical of 18th-century crewelwork. **£500–800/$800–1,300**

late 17th and early 18th centuries, trees of life and exotic birds and flowers were often included. It was also practised in France, where it was used as an alternative to silk embroidery, the designs following the style prevalent in contemporary woven silk and silk embroidery patterns.

The embroidery was taken to America by early settlers, and while in England in the second half of the 18th century crewelwork began to fall out of fashion, an independent style developed in the United States. Motifs tended to be more widely spaced than English examples, allowing more visible ground. Some have suggested that this was due to the thrifty use of the scarce woollen threads. The predominance and cheapness of indigo by the mid-18th century, introduced into South Carolina from the West Indies, meant that it was a characteristic colour, sometimes pieces being worked entirely in shades of blue against a white linen ground. In the late 18th and early 19th centuries there was a fashion for elaborate crewelwork against a black wool ground. The dyes for the wool were expensive and had to be imported, so finished examples were highly prized.

Crewelwork enjoyed a revival under the aegis of "Art Needlework" in late 19th-century Britain, although it is generally not of the quality of earlier pieces and can be readily identified. This continued into the early 20th century with the renewed interest in the Jacobean period. The 20th century has also seen the import of Kashmiri coverlets. These are worked in the style of traditional crewelwork patterns but in much softer wools, often in tambour or chain stitch, and in paler colours than the richer hues of true crewelwork coverlets

Today, crewelwork panels and coverlets command high prices on the open market, particularly 17th- and 18th-century pieces. However, it is becoming increasingly difficult to find examples in original condition. It is not generally the wools that show most wear, but the linen or cotton ground, especially when the pieces have been exposed to light or smoke during usage. This often leads to holing and splitting in the ground, and extensive restoration has to be carried out before it can be stabilized.

When considering buying a piece with restorations, the quality of this work needs to be taken into account, especially if it detracts from the original embroidery – for example, the colour of the new and original grounds being different. The freshness of the colour of the wool embroidery is also paramount.

# Care & Restoration

Determining the best possible treatment for a particular textile should be the first concern of the new owner. Each textile has to be treated individually. Should it be cleaned and preserved in its existing state? Or should it be restored, with any damaged or missing elements replaced? What do we want from the textile – will it be displayed, or stored? Is it the start of a collection, or part of a larger collection which needs a comprehensive care strategy? Investigating the textile as a whole, in particular its structure and fibres, will answer some of these questions.

One important rule to remember is that preventing deterioration with minimum intervention is best. The most important rule of all is: if in any doubt, contact a specialist. Aside from the natural ageing process, some of the worst causes of damage and deterioration are exposure to light, pollution, heat, damp, inappropriate conservation/restoration treatments, cleaning, excessive handling, mishandling, and bad storage. Once in your collection it will be easier to monitor the treatment the textile should receive.

Handling should be kept to a minimum, and the use of cotton or disposable gloves is advised, as dirt and oils from hands can cause problems. When viewing your textile, lay it out on to a flat, prepared surface, preferably covered with a clean sheet. If the textile is heavy and large get help to move it, as pulling and dragging cause stress on both the fibres and the seams. Inspect the textile for any previous repairs and restoration. These may prove to be of historic interest, and their disturbance could cause further damage and reduce its value. Costumes should not be cleaned or repaired without professional advice.

Many textiles can be cleaned by either a wet, dry or suction method, but you will need to know how to differentiate. Again, some textiles should only be cleaned by a professional, and remember some cleaning processes do more damage than good, and are irreversible. Removal of stains, rust marks and mould should be left to a specialist.

The strengths of the threads and fibres of the textile need to be investigated. Whether they are linen, wool, silk or even hemp should be determined, as should the extent of their deterioration. If there are metal threads present, use gloves, as acids from your hands can cause tarnishing. Textiles of one fibre type are easier to clean than those with mixed threads. These will have different tensions, and advice should be sought.

Never wash a textile if you are not completely sure that the colour is fast – a colourfast test must be carried out. Particular care should be taken with natural dyes, and even early chemical ones. To wash lace, whitework and other tested textiles, use only warm water. Do not wash any textile in hot water, or use detergents with bleaching agents in them. Use a net support fabric when the textile is immersed. Do not rub or squeeze; use a sponge and evenly press up and down on the textile. This will allow the suds and water to penetrate the textile and loosen the dirt. When the textile appears to be clean, drain away the water carefully, and start the rinsing process. If you are washing in a sink or bath, a shower connection is useful, as gentle movement of water above the textile will flush out the suds. All detergents must be fully removed, as they can leave a residue and attract dirt and dust back on to the textile. The final rinse should always be in distilled water. Blot the textile in an absorbent material to remove some of the excess water. All textiles should be allowed to dry flat and naturally. Pieces of lace should be pinned out carefully, on an absorbent covered pad, using brass pins only.

Textiles with glazes should not be washed. Early chintz and ikat were finished with glazes of wax or starch to make the dyes look brighter, so washing these textiles will result in the glaze being removed and the textile becoming limp with loss of colour. Modern resin finishes are now used, and these are more permanent.

Textiles such as crewelwork, tapestries and velvets, which cannot be washed, can be vacuumed. Do not vacuum fragile textiles or embroideries with sequins or beads. Use a small vacuum on low suction, and if possible clean both the back and front. The textile should always be covered with a protective net screen, and a net should always cover the vacuum head. Do not apply pressure – it is the suction that removes the dirt. Do not use the brush attachment, as this will displace loose threads.

Dirt not only causes deterioration, but also attracts insects. Good housekeeping and regular inspections are essential. The more common insects are moths, silverfish and carpet beetle. An infestation will destroy your collection very quickly, and appropriate action must be taken. Moths and other insects are becoming immune to the various chemicals used. It is not advisable to use liquid insecticides, as they can cause staining. The long-term effects of many insecticides are also not known. An alternative to chemicals is to freeze the textile, and there are specialists who do this very effectively.

## Storage
Textiles should be stored in the dark, but there should be adequate ventilation, and relative humidity of about 55 per cent. The temperature should be 5–15°C (41–59°F). Small textiles can be laid flat, with a protective sheet of acid-free tissue between each layer. Large textiles such as tapestries, banners, flags, embroidered hangings and quilts can be rolled on PVC or cardboard tubes covered with acid-free tissue. The bigger the textile, the larger the diameter of the roll should be. Roll the textile right side out and with the direction of the warp – this helps to stop crushing of the fibres. To prevent creases and folds forming in the textile, roll evenly and slowly, and always insert layers of acid-free tissue as you roll. Cover with a cotton dust sheet and secure with wide cotton tapes, tied loosely.

If there is no space available to store textiles rolled, then folding the textile is advisable. Lay the textile out as flat as possible, and pad where the fold in the material will be with tissue paper. Do not fold on earlier fold lines as this causes creasing, deterioration and weakness in the textile, and eventually holes may form. Again, cover with a cotton dust sheet. Costumes should either be stored in acid-free boxes, or hung on padded hangers with support ties. The boxes should be lined with acid-free tissue, and big enough for the costume to lie as flat as possible. Each fold should have tissue rolled in-between, to prevent creasing.

Do not squash the costume in a box that is too small, as there needs to be room for the air to circulate. If you are hanging a costume, the dust cover should be cotton, not polythene which prevents textiles from breathing and also attracts dust. Sew tapes to the waistband by hand, and loop over the hanger, so that the weight will then be supported by the tape, and not the garment. Put tissue in the sleeves to prevent folds forming.

Good storage practice can help to minimize damage. The subject of care and conservation is vast, and this is only a brief introduction. Remember that specialists are always available to help with any problems, so please use them to help safeguard your collection.

# Displaying textiles

When displaying textiles, it is important to remember that not only should the piece be visually pleasing, but that it needs to be protected from dust, insects, light, rapid temperature change and environmental pollution.

Light – both daylight and artificial light – can cause irreparable damage. The measurement of a unit of light is the "lux". The ideal light for textiles is 50 lux. This is not always achievable and some compromise may be necessary. Windows can be covered with Sun X (a clear polyester film), or a liquid ultraviolet filter, which will eliminate the most harmful rays. Closing blinds or curtains in rooms that contain your display is another way to cut down light levels. Ordinary electric light bulbs emit fewer ultraviolet rays than fluorescent lights, unless the latter have special filters.

Changes in temperature and humidity levels can weaken fibres. The ideal temperature is 13 to 14°C (56–58°F), with relative humidity of 50 to 60 per cent. This is not always possible, but try not to display your collection in too hot or dry a condition. Textiles stored too close to heat can become dry and suffer weakened fibres. Do not store or display textiles on damp walls, as this not only causes growth of mould, but can also encourage any unstable dyes to run.

Textiles can be displayed in many different ways – frames with or without glass, or display cases made from perspex, which can also have UV screening. Some larger textiles can be mounted on fabric-covered wooden stretchers, and costumes can also be displayed in cases if space permits. When framing, it is important to remember that the glass should not touch the textile. Use of acid-free fillets or a mount will prevent this. It is important that both the glass at the front and the backing of the frame are sealed correctly. If framing a larger textile, use perspex instead of glass, to avoid damage to the textile should it suffer breakage.

Whether the textile mounting is with or without glass or perspex, it will need to be secured to a prepared board. A frame can be made to the required size by a specialist framemaker, or a flat board cut to the appropriate size. This will be covered with fabric layers to stop any resins from the wood penetrating through to the textile. The textile will then be secured to the prepared board, though the method will depend on the condition of the textile. Some textiles, such as tapestries and larger pieces, can be given a strong fabric lining, with either Velcro or a sleeve for hanging. Pins, safety pins, curtain rings or any type of sharp nails should never be used for hanging any textile, even for a short period of time.

These are only a few initial thoughts and ideas on display. It is a vast subject and of great importance to the maintaining, conservation and appreciation of any textile collection.

# Useful Addresses

## MUSEUMS
### Great Britain
The American Museum in Britain, Claverton Manor, Bath BA2 7BD
Museum of Costume, Assembly Rooms, Bennett Street, Bath BA1 2QH
The Fitzwilliam Museum, Trumpington Street, Cambridge CB2 1RB
Hardwick Hall, Doe Lea, Chesterfield, Derbyshire S44 5QJ
Honiton and All Hallows Museum, High Street, Honiton, Devon EX14 8PE
British Museum, Great Russell Street, London WC1B 3DG
Victoria & Albert Museum, Cromwell Road, London SW7 2RL
Gallery of English Costume, Platt Hall, Rusholme, Manchester M14 1ES
Manchester City Art Gallery, Mosley Street, Manchester M2 3JL
Montacute House, Montacute, Yeovil, Somerset TA15 6XP
### America
Boston Museum of Fine Arts, 465 Huntington Avenue, Boston MA 02115
Art Institute of Chicago, Michigan Avenue, Chicago IL 60603
The Cleveland Museum of Art, 11150 East Boulevard, Cleveland OH 44106
Los Angeles County Museum of Art, 5905 Wilshire Boulevard, Los Angeles CA 90036
Museum of American Textile History, 800 Massachusetts Avenue, North Andover MA 01845
The Brooklyn Museum, 200 Eastern Parkway, Brooklyn NY 11238
Cooper-Hewitt National Design Museum, Smithsonian Institution, 2 East 91st Street, New York NY 10128
Metropolitan Museum of Art, 1000 Fifth Avenue, New York NY 10028-0198
Philadelphia Museum of Art, Benjamin Franklin Parkway, Philadelphia PA 19101
M.H. De Young Memorial Museum, Golden Gate Park, San Francisco CA 94118
The Textile Museum, 2320 South Street N.W., Washington D.C. 20008
### Canada
Royal Ontario Museum, 100 Queen's Park, Toronto, Ontario M5S 2C6
Museum for Textiles, 55 Centre Avenue, Toronto, Ontario M5G 2H5
### France
Musée Historique des Tissus, 30–34 rue de la Charité, 69002 Lyon
Musée du Louvre, 34–36 quai du Louvre, 75058 Paris
Musée de la Mode at du Costume, Palais Galliera, 10 Avenue Pierre 1er de Serbie, 75116 Paris

## CLUBS AND SOCIETIES
### Great Britain
The Costume Society, 21 Oak Road, Woolston, Southampton SO19 9BQ
Embroiderers' Guild, Apartment 41, Hampton Court Palace, East Molesey, Surrey KT8 9AU
The Lace Guild, 53 Audnam, Stourbridge DY8 4AE www.laceguild.demon.co.uk
The Textile Society, c/o The Victoria & Albert Museum, Cromwell Road, London SW7 2RL
### America
American Quilter's Society, P.O. Box 3290, Paducah KY 42002 www.aqsquilt.com
Costume Society of America, 55 Edgewater Drive, P.O. Box 73, Earleville MD 21919 www.costumesocietyamerica.com
Textile Society of America, P.O. Box 70, Earleville, MD 21919-0070 www.textilesociety.org
Washington Textile Group, c/o Frank Crandall, 900 Turkey Run Road, McLean VA 22101

## AUCTION HOUSES
### Great Britain
Bonhams (Knightsbridge), Montpelier Street, London SW7 1HH www.bonhams.com
Bonhams (Lots Road Galleries), 65–69 Lots Road, London SW10 ORN
Christie's (South Kensington), 85 Old Brompton Road, London SW7 3LD www.christies.com
Phillips, 101 New Bond Street, London W1Y 2AA www.phillips-auctions.com
Sotheby's, 34–35 New Bond Street, London W1A 2AA www.sothebys.com
### America
Butterfields, 220 San Bruno Avenue, San Francisco CA 94103 www.butterfields.com
Christie's, Rockefeller Centre, 20 Rockefeller Plaza, New York NY 10020 www.christies.com
Dargate Auction Houses, 5607 Baum Boulevard, Pittsburgh PA 15206 www.dargate.com
Sotheby's (New York), 1334 York Avenue at 72nd Sreet, New York NY 10021 www.sothebys.com
Sotheby's (Chicago), 215 West Ohio Street, Chicago IL 60610

## DEALERS
### Great Britain
Gallery of Antique Costume & Textiles, 2 Church Street, London NW8 8ED www.gact.co.uk

Peta Smyth Antique Textiles, 42 Moreton Street, London SW1V 2PB
Annelise Swift, Flat 7, 32 Bolton Gardens, London SW5 0AQ
Linda Wrigglesworth, Ground Floor Suite, 34 Brook Street, London W1Y 1YA
### America
America Hurrah, 230 Central Park West, New York NY 10024
Frank Ames, The Antique Textile Gallery, P.O. Box 237196, New York NY 10023 www.frankames.com
Sam Coad, Antique Textile Art Gallery, 101 West 55th Street, New York NY 10019 www.samcoad.com
James A. Ffrench, 12 East 86th Street, New York NY 10028 www.antique-oriental-carpets.com
Cora Ginsburg, 19 East 74th Street, New York NY 10021

## ANTIQUES FAIRS
### Great Britain
Textile Society Fair, Armitage Centre, Manchester (March)
The Hali Antique Carpet & Textile Art Fair, Olympia, Hammersmith Road, London W14 8UX www.halifair.com (June)
Harrogate Antiques and Fine Art Fair, Harrogate International Centre, Harrogate (May)
LAPADA Antiques Fair, The Royal College of Art, Kensington Gore, London SW7 www.lapada.co.uk (October)
Portobello Road Market, Portobello Road, London W11 (every Saturday)
### America
Baltimore Museum Antiques Show, Baltimore Museum of Art, 10 Art Museum Drive, Baltimore MD 21218
International Fine Art and Antique Dealers Show, Seventh Regiment Armory, 67th Street & Park Avenue, New York NY 10021
Philadelphia Antiques Show, 103rd Engineers Armory, 33rd & Market Streets, Philadelphia PA 19104
Washington Antiques Show, Omni Shorham Hotel, 2500 Calvert Street N.W., Washington D.C. 20008

## CONSERVATION
Textile Conservation & Restoration Studio, 24 Cholmondeley Avenue, London NW10 5XN
Conservation by Design Limited, Timecare Works, 5 Singer Way, Woburn Road Industrial Estate, Kempton, Bedford MK42 7AW
The Textile Conservancy, 40 Crooms Hill, London SE10 8HD

# Further Reading

Adamson, Jeremy, *Calico and Chintz: Antique Quilts from the Collection of Patricia S. Smith*, Washington 1997

Ames, Frank, *The Kashmir and its Indo-French Influence,* Woodbridge 1997

Aspin, Chris, *The Woollen Industry*, Princes Risborough 1994

Bath, Virginia Churchill, *Needlework in America: History, Designs and Techniques,* London 1979

Beck, Thomasina, *The Embroiderer's Story: Needlework from the Renaissance to the Present Day,* Newton Abbot 1995

Betterton, Sheila, *Quilts and Coverlets,* Bath 1978

Betterton, Sheila, *More Quilts and Coverlets,* Bath 1978

Bier, Carole, ed., *Woven from the Soul, Spun from the Heart, Textile Arts of Safavid and Qajar Iran, 16th–19th Century,* The Textile Museum, Washington1987

Bishop, Robert and Safanda, Elizabeth, *A Gallery of Amish Quilts,* New York 1976

Blum, Dilys E., *The Fine Art of Textiles,* Philadelphia 1997

Blum, Dilys E., and Haugland, H. Kristina, *Best Dressed: Fashion from the Birth of Couture to Today,* Philadelphia 1998

De Bonneville, Françoise, *The Book of Fine Linen,* New York 1994

Brett, Gerard, *English Samplers,* London 1951

Browne, Clare, *Silk Designs of the Eighteenth Century,* London and New York 1996

Browne, Clare and Wearden, Jennifer Mary, *Samplers from the Victoria & Albert Museum,* Woodbridge 2000

Bridgeman, H. and Drury, E., *Needlework: An Illustrated History,* London 1978

Bryson, Agnes F., *Ayrshire Needlework,* London 1989

Clabburn, Pamela, *Patchwork,* Princes Risborough 1983

Durant, Stuart, *The Decorative Designs of C.F.A. Voysey,* Cambridge 1990

Earnshaw, Pat, *Needlelace,* London and New York 1991

Earnshaw, Pat, *A Dictionary of Lace,* New York 1999

Earnshaw, Pat, *The Identification of Lace,* Aylesbury 1999

Edwards, Joan, *Sampler Making 1540–1940,* Dorking 1983

Fairclough, Oliver and Leary, Emmeline, *Textiles by William Morris and Morris & Co. 1861–1940,* London 1981

Farrell, Jeremy, *Umbrellas and Parasols,* London 1985

Hale, Andrew and FitzGibbon, Kate, *Ikats: Silks of Central Asia,* Woodbridge 1997

Harris, Jennifer, ed., *5000 Years of Textiles*, London 1999

Holstein, Jonathan, *Abstract Design in American Quilts,* New York 1971

Hughes, Robert, *Amish: The Art of the Quilt,* London 1994

Humphrey, Carol, *Samplers,* Cambridge 1997

Inder, P.M., *Honiton Lace,* Exeter 1971

Irwin, John, *The Kashmir Shawl,* London 1973

Irwin, John and Brett, Gerard, *Origins of Chintz: A catalogue of Indo-European cotton-paintings in the Victoria & Albert Museum, London and the Royal Ontario Museum, Toronto,* London 1985

Jones, Anita, *Patterns in a Revolution* (exhibition catalogue), The Taft Museum, Cincinatti 1990

King, Donald, *Samplers,* London 1960

Kiracofe, Rod, *The American Quilts,* New York 1993

Krody, Sumry Belger, *Flowers of Silk & Gold: Four Centuries of Ottoman Embroidery,* Washington 2000

Kumar, Rita, *Costumes and Textiles of Royal India,* New York 2000

Landi, Sheila, *The Textile Conservator's Handbook,* London 1998

Laver, James, *Costume and Fashion: A Concise History,* London 1995

Leszner, Eva Maria, *Stickmustertuçher,* Rosenheim 1985

Levey, Santina M., *Lace: A History,* London 1983

Levey, Santina M., *Elizabethan Treasures: The Hardwick Hall Textiles,* London 1998

Macey, Roy E., *Oriental Prayer Rugs,* Leigh-on-Sea 1961

Montgomery, Florence M., *Printed Textiles: English and American Cottons and Linen 1700–1850,* New York 1970

Morris, Barbara, *Victorian Embroidery,* London 1962

Orlofsky, Myron and Patsy, *Quilts in America,* New York and London 1974

Osler, Dorothy, *Traditional British Quilts,* London 1987

Parry, Linda, *Textiles of the Arts & Crafts Movement,* London and New York 1998

Reigate, Emily, *An Illustrated Guide to Lace,* Woodbridge 1986

Reilly, Valerie, *The Paisley Pattern: The Official Illustrated History,* Glasgow 1987

Ring, Betty, *Girlhood Embroidery: American Samplers & Pictorial Needle-work, 1650–1850,* New York 1993

Ring, Betty, ed., *Needlework: An Historical Survey,* Pittstown 1984

Rothstein, Natalie, ed., *Four Hundred Years of Fashion,* London 1984.

Rothstein, Natalie, ed., *Spitalfields Silks,* London 1975

Rothstein, Natalie, *Woven Textile Design in Britain from 1750–1850,* London 1994

Schoeser, Mary and Rufey, Celia, *English and American Textiles from 1790 to the Present*, New York 1989

Sichel, Marion, *History of Men's Costume,* London 1984

Sichel, Marion, *History of Women's Costume,* London 1984

Soltow, Willow Ann, *Quilting the World Over,* Radnor 1991

Stevens, Christine, *Quilts*, Cardiff 1993

Tarrant, Naomi E.A., *The Development of Costume,* London 1994

Thurman, Christa C. Mayer, *Textiles in the Art Institute of Chicago,* Chicago 1992

Tortora, Phyllis G. and Merked, Robert S., eds, *Fairchild's Dictionary of Textiles*, 7th edition, New York 1996

Trestain, Eileen, *Dating Fabrics: A Color Guide 1800–1960,* Paducah 1998.

*Samte – Velvets – Velours* (exhibition catalogue), Krefeld Textile Museum 1979

*Dentelles Européennes* (exhibition catalogue), Kyoto Modern Art Museum 1988

*Catalogue Toiles de Nantes des XVIII et XIX siecles,* Musée de l'Impression sur Etoffes, Mulhouse 1977

*Textiles in the Metropolitan Museum of Art,* New York 1995

*Cachemires Parisiens, 1810–1880* (exhibition catalogue), Palais Galliera, Paris 1998

# Glossary

**Abrash** Striations in silk or velvet colour created by the use of yarns from different batches, literally "cloud pattern".

**À disposition** Woven or embroidered to shape.

**Aesthetic Movement** Decorative arts movement with a strong Japanese influence which flourished in Europe and America from c.1860s to the late 1880s.

**Alb** Long, white vestment worn by priest.

**Aniline** Non-vegetable dye used in textile and carpet manufacture from the 1850s, which produces strong, bright colours.

**Appliqué** Technique of sewing patches on to a plain ground.

**Arabesques** Pattern of Roman origin which consists of intertwined branches, leaves and scrollwork, often arranged symmetrically.

**Art Deco** Style characterized by geometric forms and bright, bold colours, popular from c.1918 to 1940.

**Art Nouveau** Movement and style of decoration characterized by sinuous curves and flowing lines, asymmetry and flower and leaf motifs, prevalent from the 1890s to c.1910.

**Arts & Crafts Movement** An artistic movement established in the 1880s which advocated a return to quality craftsmanship and simplicity of design. William Morris was a key member.

**Atlas** Satin-faced striped fabric, usually used for kaftans or lining material, Persian.

**Au sabre** Cut velvet.

**Baroque** Extravagant and heavily ornate style of decoration and architecture that originated in 17th-century Italy. Characterized by an abundant use of cupids, cornucopia and similar decorative motifs set in curvaceous designs.

**Beadwork** Needlework in which patterns are made by sewing beads, usually of glass, to a textile ground, reaching a peak in England in the late 17th century.

**Berlin woolwork** A type of cross-stitch needlework based on published patterns originating in Berlin in the early 19th century.

**Blackwork** Used of 17th- and 18th-century embroidery worked with black thread, often on white linen, with gold and silver highlights.

**Bobbin** A turned peg on which thread is wound in lace-making. Also the shuttles used for weaving on hand looms.

**Bocha** Islamic term for square textile for wrapping precious objects.

**Bone lace** Early term for bobbin lace.

**Boteh** A traditional Islamic cone motif, adopted by European shawl manufacturers such those in Paisley.

**Braid** A band of silk, cotton, wool, gold or silver thread for trimming and binding.

**Bride** Bars or "bridges" linking individually made motifs in a lace design.

**Brocade** Weave structure employing a supplementary weft to define the pattern on the front of the textile. These strands can be seen floating on the reverse of the fabric when not used for the pattern.

**Broderie anglaise** White cut-out work with round or leaf-shaped eyelets finished with buttonhole stitches – reached its peak in the 19th century.

**Broderie perse** French term for cut-out floral and bird motifs in printed cottons and chintzes sewn on to plain quilts.

**Burlap** A coarse fabric woven from hemp or similar materials.

**Buttonhole stitch** A stitch usually worked on the edge of a piece of fabric in which a loop of thread is caught over the needle to form a small knot. These can be built up in rows free of the ground fabric.

**Calico** A cotton cloth first introduced from Calcutta in India. The term is now used in Britain to describe plain white, unprinted cotton, or in America to describe a coarse printed cotton cloth.

**Canvas work** Embroidery worked with counted stitches on an open-weave canvas.

**Cartoon** Design for carpet or tapestry often copied on to squared paper for ease of use.

**Cartouche** Decorative medallion or frame with a picture, motif or monogram.

**Chasuble** A sleeveless tunic worn by priests while celebrating Mass.

**Chenille** Silk and wool fibres wrapped around cotton or wire, popular in 18th century (French for caterpillar).

**Chiffon** A fine semi-transparent plain-weave silk fabric.

**Chiné** Warp-printed silk – European term for ikat.

**Chinoiserie** Decoration consisting of Oriental-style figures and motifs such as pagodas, pavilions, birds and lotus flowers that permeated Europe from the Far East; prevalent from the late 17th century.

**Chintz** Printed cotton, possibly a corrupted version of the Indian word chitta, or spotted cloth.

**Chintamani** Triangular arrangement of three pearls, from a traditional Buddhist emblem of three flaming pearls.

**Ciselé velvet** Uncut velvet (literally "carved") often combined with cut velvet to produce relief effect.

**Coif** Cap, usually 17th-century term.

**Cordonnet** Thread outlining clothwork or needle-lace motifs.

**Cope** Cape with simulated hood worn by priests in procession over vestments.

**Crêpe** A light fabric, usually cotton or silk, with a fine crinkled surface.

**Crewelwork** Embroidery on linen or cotton ground, can be Indian, English, French or American; named after the needle, the crewel. Often used to decorate curtains and bed-hangings in Britain and North America.

**Dalmatic** Sleeved tunic worn by priests.

**Devoré** Fabric with velvet pile removed to reveal chiffon ground.

**Diaper** Decorative pattern of repeated diamonds or other geometrical shapes.

**Drawn work** Threads drawn out of a woven fabric and embroidered over remaining threads to produce a pattern, popular in the 18th and 19th centuries.

**Droschel** Machine-made net ground.

**Edging** Narrow lace trim with one side attached to garment or textile.

**Empire style** Style inspired by the civilizations of ancient Egypt, Greece and Rome, celebrating the empire of Napoleon I (c.1804–15). It typically features such motifs as palmettes, winged lions and sphinxes. The Second Empire style refers to the revival of neo-classicism during the reign of Napoleon III (1852–70).

**Facecloth** A woven wool with a raised nap, giving the impression of felt at first glance. English wool facecloth was world famous, even turning up in Turkey and China to be worked in embroidery.

**Figuring** General term indicating silk woven with a pattern.

**Flame stitch** Stitch in chevron pattern. Also called Florentine or Bargello stitch.

**Flounce** Term for edging to lace over about 10cm (4in), usually gathered or pleated. Also called furbelows.

**Fustian** Linen and cotton mixture.

**Gobelins** Name given to the *Manufacture royale des meubles de la couronne*, established by Louis XIV in 1663 for the production of royal furnishings, especially tapestries.

**Grisaille** A technique in which the design is carried out in tones of grey, giving the effect of stonework in relief.

*Gros de Naples* High-quality French silk that imitates Italian silk.

*Gros point* Large-scale cross stitch.

**Hairwork** Late 18th- and occasionally early 19th-century embroideries worked with hair instead of embroidery silks.

*Haute couture* Made-to-measure garments bearing the designer's label.

**Herringbone** Zigzag pattern consisting of two or more rows of short parallel strokes slanting in alternating directions.

**Hollie Point** An English lace built up by forming rows of buttonhole stitch, where gaps in the rows form the pattern.

**Huguenots** French Protestants, many of whom settled in England and the Netherlands after the Revocation of the Edict of Nantes denied them religious freedom in 1685. Many were skilled silversmiths, cabinet-makers and weavers who introduced French styles into Dutch and English decorative arts.

**Ikat** Warp-printed textile of Central Asia.

**Infinite repeat** Device on rugs and carpets in which incomplete medallions are "cut" by the borders.

**Jacquard loom** A hand-loom which revolutionized the textile industry, providing a mechanical means of raising warp threads by punched cards, replacing the "draw boy", who performed this duty manually. Invented *c.* 1801 by Joseph-Marie Jacquard of Lyons.

**Japonaiserie** An exotic style practised in 19th-century Europe and derived from Japanese works of art.

*Jugendstil* German and Austrian term for the Art Nouveau style. Named after the Munich-based publication *Jugend*.

*Kalimkari* Traditional Persian printed silk (literally "penwork").

*K'esi* or *kossu* Tapestry-woven silk.

**Lampas** A weave structure which uses two sets of warps and wefts to form patterns. One set is usually a foundation warp and weft, anchoring the colours of the second set.

**Lappets** Pair of tapering lace strips, 5–10cm (2–4in) in length, hanging from lady's cap and framing face.

**Lawn** A fine, translucent linen material.

**Linen** A strong fabric spun from fibres of the flax plant. Also a generic term for clothes, sheets, tablecloths and other household items.

**Maniple** Stole worn by priest.

*Mehrab* Niche facing Mecca in a mosque, on both mats and wall-hangings (also called prayer arch).

**Mezzara** Elegant 19th-century Genoese cotton voile with Indian-inspired pattern of flowering tree.

**Moiré** Watered silk.

**Mordant** Substance applied before dye to help fix colour in fabric.

**Neo-classicism** Mid- to late 18th-century style of architecture and decoration based on the forms of ancient Greece and Rome. Typical elements include classical motifs such as garlands of flowers, palmettes, husks, vases, urns, key patterns and mythical creatures.

*Opus Anglicanum* Medieval ecclesias-tical embroidery of extremely high quality worked in English convents.

**Orphrey** Embroidered panel in the shape of a cross on chasubles and other ecclesiastical vestments.

*Palampore* Indian bedcover with tree of life design, imported into Europe from the 17th century.

*Pallu* Patterned end-borders to Indian shawls or saris.

**Patchwork** Textile made by piecing together scraps of fabric, often used for making quilts.

*Patola* Silk sarong produced in Gujarat for the Indonesian market.

*Pashmina* Fine Kashmir wool (see *Shah tus*).

*Petit point* Small-scale cross stitch.

**Plushwork** A raised, tufted stitch popular in the mid-19th century.

**Provenance** Documented history of any antique item, passed on to each new owner. An unusual or notable provenance may enhance the value of a piece.

**Quilting** A method of sandwiching a layer of wadding between two layers of cloth, which are then stitched in place by quilting stitches – generally used on bedcovers.

**Repoussé** Relief decoration on metal hammered from reverse side.

*Réseau* The background of the lace design. In most needle laces this is made later and connected to individual pieces of *toilé*; in bobbin laces it is generally made as one piece with the *toilé*.

*Reticella* An early needle lace with open-work patterns and buttonhole stitching on linen, popular in Italy in the 16th and 17th centuries.

**Satin stitch** Straight stitch laid in parallel to imitate sheen of satin.

**Selvedge** The lateral border of a loom length of silk. It can be striped, strengthened with cotton, or of contrasting colour to the main body of the textile, and is a useful tool in dating.

**Shagreen** Untanned leather, originally the skin of the shagri, a Turkish wild ass, but now used to include sharkskin.

*Shah tus* Finest Kashmir wool, literally "King's wool" – finer than *pashmina*.

**Smocking** Gathering material into pleats, sewn together by a variety of decorative stitches.

**Stomacher** A roughly triangular panel, frequently embroidered, forming the front of open robes of the 16th century on, often decoratively laced.

**Strapwork** Decorative ornament resembling a series of thongs, rings and buckles which was used mainly in the 16th and 17th centuries and revived in the 19th century.

**Stumpwork** Victorian term denoting raised needlework on a ground of cotton or cotton wool, often mounted as pictures. Popular during the 17th century, now generally known as raised work.

**Sumptuary laws** Laws forbidding the import, ownership or manufacture of luxury goods.

**Swags** Decoration of hanging chains of flowers, husks or fabrics.

**Swatch** Sample of fabric.

**Tapestry** Woven in tapestry technique on high looms; same technique used to produce Kashmir shawls.

**Tester** Canopy or ceiling over a bed.

**Toile** Cotton or linen fabric, particularly for furnishing.

*Toilé* The pattern or clothlike portion in both bobbin and needle laces.

**Treen** Turned wooden objects.

**Trelliswork** Geometric decoration in the form of a lattice.

*Trompe l'oeil* Pictorial decoration intended to deceive the eye.

**Voile** Transparent muslin.

*Vraie réseau* Handmade net.

**Warp** Vertical (lengthwise) threads in a woven textile. These threads form the framework for woven cloth. They are strung on the loom first; the weft is then threaded through.

**Weft** Horizontal threads in foundation of woven textile, interwoven with the warps.

**Whitework** Embroidery worked with a white thread on a white ground, favoured since the Middle Ages for articles of church use and for linen.

**Worsted** Glazed (unwashed) tweed.

**Yastik** The cover of a cushion or bolster (Ottoman).

# Index

# Acknowledgments

Author's Acknowledgments

I would like to thank everyone who gave me their valuable time. Particular thanks go to Clare Brown of the Victoria & Albert Museum, and Susan Mayor, Suzette Shields and Fariba Thomson of Christie's. Thanks also to Robin Milne for his invaluable assistance. Judy Wentworth, Titi Halle, Alison Toplis, Christopher Lennox Boyd and Meg Andrews were all of great help in tracing elusive facts and images.